THE TWELVE

PRINCIPLES

OF

OPTIMAL LIVING

LIZ ADAMSON

THE TWELVE PRINCIPLES OF OPTIMAL LIVING.

by Liz Adamson

Published by Diviniti Publishing Ltd
83, Birling Rd, Leybourne, Kent ME19 5HZ
Tel: 01732 220373
Email admin@hypnosisaudio.com
Website: www.hypnosisaudio.com

ISBN 1 901923 42 8

1st Edition

Cover Image by Diane Frost

INTRODUCTION

I decided to write this book in order to provide a simple guide to help people to understand how life works and give ways to put this guidance into action. Life is to be enjoyed. It is an incredible journey of growth, adventure and enlightenment. This is, of course, an ideal that very few people actually experience. The reality more often is of struggle, pain, both physical and emotional and of survival. The disparity between these two experiences is due to the fact that we are not taught how to achieve the ideal or even that it is an option. We learn from our parents and other members of society how to repeat the patterns that create struggle. Even when we try to break away from our original patterning we usually end up creating it in a different guise.

There are a few truths and principles that if understood and adhered to can totally transform our lives, leaving behind the pain and struggle and creating the joy and enlightenment that is our birthright. Life is incredibly simple and works magically when we apply the basic principles. Many religions try to give us a set of rules to live by but built into these are elements like fear, guilt, blame, elitism and punishment. These have no part to play in the principles of optimal living and will indeed block this state.

My intention in putting these principles together is to state clearly and simply the truths that we can use to make the most of the wonderful opportunities that life in this world has to offer. The result of this is that we are happy, fulfilled, loved and loving, abundant, creative and empowered. We can find and live up to the potential that is our birthright and that can be used for the good of all.

I will also give very practical ways of applying the truths to everyday aspects of life and living so they don't become too lofty for us to aspire to. Sometimes we think we are too busy living our everyday lives to work on ourselves. We may perceive that we have to take a course, or have the time and space to focus on our own issues. However, the reality is that our schoolroom is sitting in traffic, having a row with the boss or being driven mad by demanding children. It is how we deal with these things that determine whether we are using the principles to our advantage.

There are enormous rewards to be reaped from following and living by these principles. These are often instantaneous and can be very dramatic. Our outer world is merely a reflection of what we think, feel and believe internally. Consequently, any changes made on an inner level will have an effect on what we experience on an external level. Our relationships improve, we are able to attract more abundance, we notice that synchronistically amazing things happen to move us forward or to give us what we need.

These principles are not things that we do once and the lesson is learned. They need to be integrated deep into our beings. At first we will need to be aware of applying them but after a while they become second nature and firmly established as part of who we are.

Part of this process is to be aware in advance of where and how we do not live these principles and be prepared to establish these new ways as and when they arise. If we do not do this, we will find that we simply act in the moment as we have done before. When we know what pushes our buttons or the patterns that we keep repeating, we can prepare in advance how we will think, feel and act the next time we are faced with these circumstances.

Many of the principles tie in with Universal Law. These are not laws or rules such as we encounter within society or the church. There are no punishments as such for not adhering to them. In a way they are the natural laws of energy. When we understand and work within these laws, everything flows to our advantage. When we go against the laws, the energy is not able to flow and we find ourselves in a state of struggle. There is no one and nothing standing over us and judging whether we deserve to be punished or rewarded, other than our own egos of course.

I trust that these principles may make as much difference in your life as they have in mine. Good luck on your journey to transformation!

These are the Twelve Principles

Principle No. 1
RECLAIM YOUR
PERSONAL POWER

RECLAIM YOUR
PERSONAL POWER

NO ONE CAN TAKE OUR POWER
FROM US WE CAN ONLY GIVE IT AWAY

Power is a very emotive word and many of us are not comfortable with the concept of personal power. Perhaps we have an inkling as to just how powerful we are and are afraid of the responsibility that accompanies this.

First, I need to differentiate between external and inner personal power. Virtually all the examples we have of power would involve the former. We see it in politicians, dictators and those with money, status or position that can be wielded over other people. We may associate this sort of power with corruption or sleaze. Those with external power will often render other people powerless. Those who seek external power will often do so because they are not in touch with their own inner power.

Personal power does not seek to dominate or negatively affect others; indeed, it will work to empower those around us. Our personal power will generate the energy needed to create what we need and want in our lives. If we do not have this we may feel stuck or stagnant. Nothing happens and we may well be tired and apathetic a great deal of the time. The less energy we have to send out, the less will be able to come back to us in the form of opportunities, miracles and gifts.

We are not taught as children how to deal with our own personal power, or even of its existence. In an ideal world children need to be comfortable with the amount of power they have within the family. Parents need to set clear and firm boundaries. Within these boundaries the child has complete power and autonomy. As the child gets older the boundaries extend further in a gradual way so that the child feels secure with the added scope for their power. When it is ready to fly the nest, it is then able to cope with its personal power and how to use it in the world. If parents are too strict, the child learns to give its power away in the hope of getting love and approval back in return. If we are too liberal or our boundaries are inconsistent, we may give our power away to the child who wields it as destructive external power. We have all seen children who would give Hitler a run for his money. These parents are completely dominated and controlled by the whims of the child. Children are not developed enough to know how to cope with too much power and will often be very unpopular with both adults and children alike.

We often give our power away to someone if we want something from them in return. This is never more true than in relationships. In the early "in love" phase of the partnership, we may give our power away in the hope that we get love back. From this point on we may try to get our power back within the relationship. However, we do this by wielding external power, which is very destructive. We may manipulate and control, we could withhold things we know our partner wants from us, we may be competitive and try to score points off each other. This resulting power struggle will often sound the death knell of the relationship and we still feel completely powerless at the end of it.

We can clearly see the patterns with power in the issue of bullying. A bully is someone who feels powerless and insecure inside and compensates for these feelings by trying to obtain external power. A bully will usually choose a victim who already has a pattern of giving his or her power away. They rarely dominate someone who is secure in their personal power. Remember that bullying is not just something that happens at school but is very prevalent in the adult world as well. This form of bullying is often more subtle; the person will often get themselves into a role that has some external power like a boss or chairman of a committee or captain of a sports team. People give their power to this person because it seems easier than standing up to them. There is usually a hook that is needed as well. The person may be very efficient and has made themselves indispensable: they may provide the refreshments or finance some aspect of the group or be able to sack us. When there is a group dynamic, it can be difficult if other members of the group back the bully out of their own fear. The bully works with and feeds off the power given to it by other people. Without that power they are nothing.

The biggest thing that we give our power away to is our own ego. This is like a parasite that lives and feeds off us. It in turn feeds us our fears, our insecurities, our needs, our lack, our judgements, our guilt, anger, hurt, jealousy etc. All of these things are born out of an illusion that we have made real by how we have chosen to perceive the circumstances of the past. The most common illusions that we buy into are that we are not good enough or undeserving. When we give our power and energy to something, we manifest it in our lives. Every time we believe the ego propaganda machine and think that we or others are less or more, we give power to the ego, which may use it very destructively or abusively. The more empowered our ego becomes, the more chaotic our lives will be to reflect this to us. Reclaiming our power back from the ego is a long term and ongoing process. However, the rewards for doing this are huge and instant. Once we get the ego down to a manageable size, it becomes easy to deal with its more subtle ploys. If we do not feel good, creative, abundant and fulfilled then the ego is overpowering our true Divine selves.

It takes a great deal of commitment and discipline to disempower the ego. It will be very wily in its tactics and often creeps up on us when we are not in a state of awareness. It is very clued in on our weak spots and Achilles' heel and it will constantly play on these. Each time we are aware that once again we have given our power away to the ego, we can still recall it and disempower the ego.

Most of us do not want others to give us their power; it is very uncomfortable and a huge responsibility. When someone puts us on a pedestal and thinks the world of everything we do or are, they give us their power. They elevate us above our natural level and place themselves below us. They do not think that they are worthy in comparison to us. They do not realise that it is only their power that appears to raise us above them and if they withdraw it we come tumbling down. We can see the pattern occur with celebrities and sports stars. Personal power knows that we are all equal and our job in the world is to raise others up to the highest common denominator.

Those people who do want to take the power that we give them will usually end up using it against us or abusing us with it. These people often choose jobs or roles in life that put them in a position of authority where they can take power with impunity.

We often lose sight of the fact that the most powerful people are actually the masses, the ordinary people. Politicians and people in high office are only there because we put them there and consequently we can also remove them. They are our servants and representatives and if they are not serving us in the way that we want them to, we can do something about it.

People power is an incredible force. It can change the world, stop war and make a massive difference. We can combine our personal power and make a stand. We have seen this work in the area of GM foods and to an extent in the nuclear weapons arena. If only we could become more universally aware of the extent of our people power, we could use it more fully. It was surely people power that brought down the iron curtain. In my work I constantly seeing people who have been sexually, physically or emotionally abused in childhood. In virtually every case I asked them what happened to make the abuse stop and the answer is "I said no." In that moment they began to take back their power and the abuser was unable to continue. We need to learn that we have this amazing word at our disposal that does not allow people to take our power because we are not choosing to give it away.

The golden rule of personal power is NEVER SPEND THE CAPITAL, ONLY USE THE INTEREST. This means that we do not give away our power because if we do, we deplete the amount of energy that our incredible power-house is able to generate. It would be like giving away the goose that lays the golden egg one piece at a time but still wanting to have the gold. When our personal power is working at full production, it is quite incredible. There are very few people who are fortunate enough to experience this. The fact is that we have probably given away little bits of our power to a variety of people during our lives. The more we give away, the less we have working for us. In extreme cases we give so much of our power away that we become victims and allow others to totally dictate our lives. Victims feel powerless to make changes or decisions and often stay stuck in abusive relationships or dire circumstances because they feel paralysed by their lack of power. It is important to note that as we reclaim our power and use it to our best advantage, this may seem to threaten those who are not in their own power or are trying to obtain external power. The jealousy aimed at us may seem to be a reason to hide our power. **DO NOT DO THIS.** Understand where the other person is coming from without taking on board their insecurity. It is their issue and not ours. It is essential that we do not become afraid of our own power and consequently try to tone it down to a level that makes others feel comfortable with their own lack of power. There is a huge peer pressure to be normal or as others are and not to stand out in a crowd. If we are to help lead others to find their personal power, we have to have done it first.

Part of the process of reclaiming our personal power is to take back the power that we have given away to people in the past. It may feel as if it is too late to do this as what is done is done. However, in the inner self, all time is one and we can undo anything that we have done. Every time we have felt powerless in a situation, we have given our power away.

The centre of personal power in the body is the solar plexus. It is called this because there is a vast network of nerves that come together at this point that resembles the rays of the sun. This is quite a good metaphor to use with our personal power. Just as with the sun, it radiates energy that promotes life. We exist on the heat and light that is generated from this power centre. When we reclaim our personal power, we want to focus on the solar plexus and reactivate this amazing personal generator.

REASONS WHY WE GIVE OUR POWER AWAY

1) We want people to like or love us.
2) We are afraid.
3) We think we are unworthy or not good enough.

4) We think the other person is or has more than us.

5) We are dependent on them and don't want to lose what they provide for us.

6) We feel guilty if we say no.

7) We want praise or approval.

8) We want others to take responsibility for our lives.

9) We want a quiet life and think that we get it by giving in. (**WRONG!**)

10) We feel sorry for or are trying to protect the other person.

TAKING BACK POWER

1) Ask the unconscious mind to tell you what percentage of your potential personal power you have given away. Take a deep breath and let the number show itself to you. Do not try to think this number or figure it out logically. This number will be the amount you need to take back from people in the past. Do not let the ego give you this number. Most people are working at 10% or less of their potential power.

2) Make a list of people that you have given your power to, starting with the most recent. The most likely candidates will be relationships, friends, work colleagues or bosses, siblings, parents, teachers, neighbours, people in authority, bullies, abusers and burglars. You may be surprised how long this list is. Note if any of these people gave their power to you, if so you will want to give it back. This occurs particularly in relationships. Look at where you perhaps needed to say NO long before you did.

3) Do each individual separately. Look at the ways in which you gave each person your power. Refer to the list of ways. There may be more than one reason.

4) Remove yourself from any distractions. Sit comfortably and close your eyes. Take some deep breaths to relax the body and slow down the mind's chatter. When you feel calm and centred, conjure up the image or sense of this person from whom you are reclaiming your power. See them a few feet in front of you. Command your inner self to recall and revoke any power that you have given away to this person. You may want to activate a symbolic magnet in the solar plexus. See the power coming back to you as golden globules like liquid mercury. These all join together in the solar plexus. Feel yourself becoming stronger and more energised as this happens, you body language may reflect this as you stand in your power. Give back any power that the other person may have given to you. This can be done by handing them a symbol of the power. Check out if there are any unhealthy attachments still in place with them and cut yourself free from these. If this person is no longer in your life, release them with love and watch them fade away. If the person has abused you or made you be or do something that you did not want, then see yourself standing in your power and saying NO.

5) As you go back in time reclaiming your power from people in your past, see or sense yourself at the age you were when you gave your power to this person. This is quite important as you have all ages living within you and if your 5 or 12 year old is still feeling powerless, this will have a knock on effect in your adult life.

6) There may be people from the past that you have buried deep in your unconscious. Simply clear these as and when you become aware of them.

7) Check your power percentage.

RECLAIMING POWER FROM THE EGO

1) It may help to give yourself some kind of visual image to represent the ego. This may be a worm, snake or parasitic creature, or an imp, monster, gremlin or devil. Go with what feels comfortable.

2) When you become aware of some ego propaganda or not feeling good due to being in the ego state, ask what you are feeling, thinking or believing to bring you into this mode.

3) Regardless of whether this thing has become a reality or not, ask yourself whether you want this to be true or if it serves you in who you **WANT** to be.

4) If the answer to this is no, then command your inner and unconscious self to delete this particular belief or reality. If there is an emotion attached like fear, anger, hurt, guilt, shame or jealousy, expel them from the body using the breath.

5) See the ego in its symbolic form and command the inner self to recall and revoke any power or energy that has been given to this thing. See the ego shrink as the golden energy you gave it returns to your solar plexus.

6) Each time you do this you will lessen the power the ego has over you and you will be able to choose in each moment what you want to think, feel or believe rather than be governed by what the ego has chosen to perceive in the past.

7) Remember that the ego has a positive role to play in showing us our old and unworkable patterns and beliefs. As we reduce its power, we can see it as a

loveable but naughty puppy that we can laugh at.

TIPS FOR MAINTAINING POWER

1) If someone is manipulative, do not play the game. They can only control you if you give them the power to do so. Use the magic word. Say NO.

2) Maintaining power does not mean getting into a power struggle or conflict. This will only serve to disperse your resources. Feel the inner resolve and intention and stick by your guns. Once again if you do not choose to play the power game, it does not mean that the other person wins. The other person will be trying to obtain external power from you and can do nothing if you do not let them.

3) Look at the needs you have that allow you to give your power away to others in order that they may meet your needs. Do you need love, approval, material security, companionship etc. Look at how you can be responsible for obtaining these things without needing them from others who may be unwilling to give them consistently.

4) Do you have an issue with authority figures? Do you feel guilty if you see a police car or traffic warden? Do you dread having to go and see your child's head teacher? When this occurs, take back your power and remind yourself that these people are working for you. They are public servants and you are the public.

5) If there is a world or domestic issue that you feel strongly about, do not think that you are powerless to make changes. Talk to your friends and see if they feel similarly. The collective energy and power of ordinary people can move mountains.

6) Learn to be comfortable with the full extent of your power. Do not hide it or worry if other people feel threatened by it. The more powerfully your light shines, the more hope there is for mankind.

7) Teach others to find, maintain and reclaim their power. These may be your children, partners, friends and colleagues. This is done mainly by example and encouragement. When others see what works for you, they can follow suit.

8) When dealing with the family, e.g. parents, siblings, spouses and children, there may be old patterns of giving power away. These patterns need to be broken each time they surface. Be aware of what you have done in the past that gave your power away and know in advance how to do it differently next time. The NO word may need to be employed. For instance, your daughter is always getting you to baby-sit to the extent that she is always out and you have no life. You would want to have a ready phrase to hand next time you are asked like "No. I'm sorry its not convenient." Note that as soon as you feel you have to justify yourself or find an excuse, you give your power away. Nor should you ever give in to any emotional blackmail.

9) You can give your power to inanimate things like the house, garden, job, hobbies, addictions or illnesses. If these things are controlling you rather than the other way round, you are going to be rendered powerless.

The benefits to reclaiming our personal power are endless. We have more energy, we are not afraid, we get our needs met and we feel centred, happy and peaceful. We are also able to pass the rewards on to those around us.

Principle No. 2
GO WITH
THE FLOW

GO WITH THE FLOW

"Go with the flow" is a phrase that is bandied around a great deal and yet this concept is one, which, if lived by, will provide untold bounty and rewards. It may have a slightly hippie connotation, a hangover from the sixties. consequently, we may not take it too seriously and not have a real idea of the full implications of this principle.

Going with the flow is one of the most important things we can learn to do. Sadly, we do have to learn this or, it might be truer to say, to unlearn the things that make us go against the flow. It is actually the most natural thing in the world for us to do. Virtually every baby is at one with the flow of life; they do not know how to be any different. Gradually life, parents, teachers and society reverse this so that most adults are trying to swim upstream a great deal of the time.

Going with the flow means that we work with the rhythms, cycles and energy of life and not against it. Everything in the world is made up of energy and there are certain laws that govern energy. Whether we like it or not, these same laws will apply to every area of our lives since we are composed of energy. If the energy in our physical body is not allowed to flow, we will get ill. If our emotions are not flowing then this will create problems in our lives and relationships. If the circuitry of the brain is impaired, then this will have a knock on effect. If our spiritual energy is not able to flow, we are deprived of the love, help and guidance that are available to us. The fact is that if we block the flow of energy then nothing will work properly. The good news is that we don't have to make the flow happen, we have only to make sure that we do not get in its way. As soon as we can understand how energy works and how we can work with it then our lives will reflect this in positive ways.

If we use the image of the river of life, we are on rafts and we have the choice as to whether we relax and allow the tidal flow to carry us, without knowing where it will take us, or, we can get our paddles out and take charge and control and put vast amounts of effort into taking our rafts upstream against the tide. If we go for this option, we may find that we end up staying in the same place and we have used up a great deal of personal energy to do this. Sometimes we see people who use a huge amount of determination and energy and who may manage to propel their rafts a bit further ahead but if they let up this effort, the tide will bring them back again. If we are allowing our rafts to flow along the river of life, we will find that we come across others flowing in the same direction and at the same speed as us. We become fellow travellers for as long as our speed and direction are compatible. If this changes, we wish them well and carry on our way without any negative residue. This applies to our relationships and friendships in life.

The main sign that we are going against the flow of life is that we are in a state of struggle. It may seem as if we are putting a great deal of effort in and yet only managing to survive or to maintain the status quo. When we are in struggle, we will feel tired a great deal of the time, as there is very little energy left with which to enjoy and make the most of life. When we are in struggle, it may feel as if we are being knocked back by circumstances, jobs or deals falling through or not working out as planned. There may be a great deal of disillusion and stress created. One area in which many people experience struggle is financial. This is because money is simply an energy and if it is not allowed to flow, it will not come to us. For some people the harder they struggle to get or earn more money, the more it seems to be swallowed up in bills, rent, mortgages, debts or the essentials of life. There does not seem to be enough for the luxuries without going deeper into debt. We can certainly see this pattern playing out when we spend on credit; many people only manage to pay back the interest each month and are on a treadmill that becomes very difficult to get off. We are also made to feel guilty for the money that we spend on nonessentials or treats for ourselves.

Struggle has sadly become the norm for many people in today's world, so much so that we often don't even recognise or question it. If everyone else is in the same position, then we think that this is how life is and we simply have to get on with it. There is such a huge pressure on us to conform and be like everyone else that we don't necessarily look for another better way. Indeed, when we come up against the minority who have learned to go with the flow, we can be very quick to brand them as weirdoes and make them wrong for what they are doing. This merely perpetuates the struggle and puts others off from breaking away from the norm and being different.

Often our struggles involve trying to gain external power. We want the position, the money, the status or are trying to create a sense of perfection in our lives. If these things are not incorporated into our personal flow, we have to struggle to obtain them. Things that are achieved through struggle are often not long lived. Even if we do not lose what we have gained, there might be a fear of loss or more struggle involved in maintaining our gains and this may spoil any enjoyment that we may get.

Society reinforces our patterns of struggle. We have beliefs like "no pain, no gain" or "You have to work hard to get where you want to be." We don't like it if people appear to succeed without putting much effort into it. We devalue their achievements and rewards. We may also think that life or God should reward us for our struggles. It is this understanding that keeps many people stuck in the struggle. Society also puts a huge emphasis on success. Our very being is measured by this very dubious external quality. The desire and need for success is one of our biggest motivational forces. It is the thing that keeps us swimming upstream towards this goal. Success in society is measured by things like money, trophies, cars, homes, being the best, rank, position and how much others envy or admire us for all of the above.

THE ONLY MEASURE OF SUCCESS THAT COUNTS IS THE DEGREE OF INNER PEACE, HARMONY AND HAPPINESS THAT WE ACHIEVE.

Society also reinforces the belief that if we want something, we have to make it happen. If we have enough drive and determination, we can get it. While this may be true in some cases, it is often a very empty achievement. If this thing was not on our path and we had to expend vast amounts of energy in order to get it, it will not provide us with the satisfaction or fulfilment we require. This same amount of energy could be invested in things that will bring a good return on our investment and have a positive outcome for all concerned. This will happen as a matter of course if we are going with the flow.

Control is a clear indication that we are in struggle and going against the flow. This applies whether we are the one doing the controlling or allowing ourselves to be controlled. Control has become a massive and destructive problem in the world. We see it at all stages and in every area of life. Men and women are both equally susceptible to this pattern. In order for control to work there has to be a hook. There needs to be something we want, or don't want to lose, like love, a job or financial or material benefits. Without the hook, the control freak has no ammunition to keep us tied to them. Both sides of the control equation are coming from a position of powerlessness. The controller will try to gain external power to make up for this sense of powerlessness. The controllee will think itself too powerless to stand up to them and may believe any propaganda put forward by the controller. There is usually a great deal of fear at work within this pattern on both sides.

Where there is a need for control there have often been past situations where those who we trusted to be there for us have either let us down or hurt us. When this occurs, we learn that we cannot trust anyone and therefore we have to use control in order to feel safe from being hurt again. Control will usually end up reinforcing the hurts; people don't like us or feel comfortable with us. In relationships the control will often break up the partnership or be so very destructive. Control will never work as a life strategy and it will block the good things that the flow of life has to offer. It may be necessary to go back and heal the factors that have given birth to our need for control.

✳ When we go against the flow, we put ourselves on a treadmill that never seems to get us anywhere. Many people can identify with this. Their lives follow very rigid patterns. They may struggle to get up in the morning, struggle to commute to work, spend the day stressfully sorting out problems or keeping up with a huge work load, they then struggle to get home again where they are too tired to do more than eat, watch television and go to bed. Weekends will be catching up with all the jobs that they didn't have the time or energy to do in the week. This is the reality for a great many people. In order to cope with this, we often become virtual robots. We suppress our dreams and creativity, and we suppress our passions and our connection with the inner self. When we get stuck in this kind of a rut or pattern, our higher selves will often try to get through to us to make the changes to put us back on track and in the flow. Our egos and logical mind will usually override any of these suggestions. How would we make money? The family is dependent on us. How would we survive? When we do not listen to the inner voice, we might attract something altogether more insistent. This is what I call the "cosmic kick up the bum." It will push us off the treadmill and force us to revaluate our lives. Cosmic kicks may come in the form of an illness such as cancer, stroke, heart problems or a nervous breakdown. Bad backs or broken limbs often figure in this. They can also be something like redundancy, bankruptcy or divorce. All these things may be undesirable and yet they will be the catalyst that completely reshapes our lives and, if heeded, can put us back in the flow. It is important to note that these extreme challenges can be avoided by listening to the inner voice or intuition and by following the guidance given in the first place. This will be given to us many times over before the stronger action may need to be taken. If we have buried our heads in the sand, we may not have taken this on board. ✳

Sometimes life tries to prevent us from going against the flow. However, many of us would not recognise this at the time. We may go down many dead end alleys in our lives that temporarily take us off our path. This may be jobs or relationships that will not amount to anything. The higher self will watch as we go down that route only to discover that it is not right for us and we then return to the path and try something else. We are at a point in our evolution where there is no time to waste on things that are not on our path or part of our destiny. Consequently, doors that do not lead us to where we are meant to go will often be closed to us. This may seem very disheartening. If we are set on a particular outcome, it will tap into our insecurities and fears of failure. This is an illusion. **IF A DOOR DOES NOT OPEN FOR US EASILY, THEN IT IS THE WRONG DOOR.** We will find that when we try to push the right door, it opens effortlessly and everything works like clockwork. This is the sign we need to know that we are on the right track.

Everything in our lives is meant to be easy. If it is not, it is once again a sign that we are not going with the flow. Society does not teach us that things are meant to be easy. It will be more inclined to lead us to expect difficulties along the way. If what we are doing is not easy then it is either the wrong thing for us or we are going about it the wrong way or the timing is not right. Whichever option we are buying into, struggle will be created. It is important to be aware when we are experiencing difficulties we may need to stop and ask ourselves whether this is the right thing for us. If the answer from the inner self is a categorical yes, then we need to look at how we are going about it or whether we are jumping the gun. Look for guidance or accept that it will happen in the right time and place.

Another huge block to going with the flow is our emotions. Our negative feelings can be extremely heavy and we carry them around with us like a mass of baggage. Sometimes our emotions weigh down the raft of life to such an extent that we are grounded and cannot move forward or back. Our lives don't seem to go anywhere; we are always tired and apathetic or we stagnate. This state of affairs applies to a great many people. They are not necessarily in struggle but they are not moving forward either. The big four negative emotions are fear, anger, hurt and guilt. These are the main culprits in keeping us stuck. If we are to refloat our raft and get moving, we have to ditch the baggage of our negative emotions. This is done one bag at a time. Each time something comes along that triggers an emotion, we are able to throw out this bag. As we ditch these things, we become lighter and we will find that we are able to move faster along our path, achieving more along the way. The same also applies to aspects of our past that we have not let go of. This could be old relationships, an injustice or a loss that we have suffered. For all these things we only need to carry forward the lessons or gifts these things were there to provide and release all other aspects.

The thing that keeps us in struggle and therefore going against the flow is the ego. This is the voice at the back of our mind that will feed us our fears and all the terrible things that will happen if we decide to give up the struggle. It will show us all sorts of negative scenarios that if we believe, will keep us struck in the old patterns. The ego always gives us illusions but it will know how to play to our insecurities. It will remind us of the times in the past when we have suffered or gone through difficulties and tells us this is what will happen if we do not listen to it. If we believe the ego and give it our power, we will remain on the treadmill and be unable to partake in all the amazing opportunities that life has to offer.

It is our intuition that will be our guide to finding and going with the flow. Our intuitive voice may be much more subtle than the ego voice. Even when we get a clear message from our inner selves, the ego will often override it with its propaganda. We often choose to go with what we are used to experiencing rather than go into new uncharted territory. The fact is that our intuition will be giving us the guidance needed whether we listen to it or not. The intuition works through feelings rather than thoughts, it is the gut feeling that many people describe. Our intuition will NEVER give us bad advice or try and steer us toward a place we would not want to go. When we trust this knowledge, we can begin to see that if we disregard it, there will be consequences that we might not want. I must make it clear that this is not a punishment for not listening, simply the result.

Along our path of life there are signposts that lead us to the next point. We need to access and use our intuition to show us which are the genuine signposts and which are red herrings. We might be reading an article or classified advertisements and something jumps out at us. Our role is to follow up on the information and see where it takes us. Our signposts come in a great many different guises and the trick is to recognise them. For instance, you might have been in a job that is not satisfactory but it is safe. A new boss arrives who makes your life a misery. He may be the signpost you need to leave that job and find something new.

The first thing we need to do to give up the struggle and go with the flow is to give up the fight and SURRENDER. The ego will tell us that if we do this, we have lost and we will be destroyed. This is not correct, any sense of a battle was always an illusion. When we surrender, we hand over the reins and control to our higher selves and there will be a change of direction. This may seem strange at first, it is not what we are used to. Part of going with the flow is not knowing where or what the flow is going to take us to. Many of us are very goal orientated and this aspect may not be very appealing. Giving up goals or changing them for much more airy-fairy objectives can be a challenge.

Where struggle is a sign that we are against the flow, coincidences, synchronicity and miracles are signs that we are going with it. Some coincidences may be part of the signpost network, while others have no apparent message or benefit to provide. When this occurs it is often just for confirmation that we are on track and heading in the right direction. These are our "cosmic pats on the back." Miracles are a very natural part of life. When we are on the right path, they can be a daily occurrence and are our natural birthright. They do not tend to feature much when we are in struggle though and once again they can be a confirmation that we have let the struggle go.

There are a great many cycles and rhythms with which we need to flow. Some of these are our own personal biorhythms and cycles; we feel better and have more energy at certain times than at others. We also need to tune into the cycles of nature, the seasons, the lunar and planetary fluctuations and the weather etc. We can take advantage of the benefits that each different thing has to offer. For instance, during spring and summer months we may have more energy and want to be out and about and mix with friends or doing sports and in autumn and winter we want to stay in and be cosy indoors. Both have advantages to offer. All energy oscillates, there will be peaks and troughs and we need to go with this roller coaster ride always knowing that a peak will follow a trough just as day follows night.

Expectations will always result in a sense of disappointment. We often create a whole list of things that we expect from life. This may be in our relationships, our careers, our standard of living, etc. We have to let go of all expectations when we go with the flow. We have no idea what lies beyond the next bend and if we have an expectation as to what this "should" be, we will not get the full benefit of what is on offer. Once we can trust that we might not get what we expect, we can get something that is better for us in the long run.

One of our most basic motivations is to get our needs met. We often have a whole list of these that we expect people or situations to fulfil. When we go with the flow, we hand over our needs to a higher power to meet. We will not know what or why we need something until it arrives. It may be a person, some knowledge or a course, a book, a windfall, a job or a change of direction. We simply trust that all our needs are met and wait and see what turns up. We may only realise the significance of what we get at a later date when we see the whole sequence of events and where they lead.

We often hear that it is the journey and not the destination that is important. This is very true. To get the most from the journey we have to stay in the moment. We cannot know what is ahead so there is little point in speculating. Equally, we do not want to carry our past with us or keep harping back to it. Staying in the moment is often a skill that we can learn. It involves putting the focus of our attention on what is going on around us and not getting caught up with the thinking mind. There is so much beauty and bounty that can be missed if we do not take the trouble to notice it.

SIGNS THAT WE ARE NOT GOING WITH THE FLOW

1) Struggle and resistance.

2) Feeling stuck or blocked.

3) Tiredness and apathy.

4) A need to control or allowing yourself to be controlled.

5) A desire to make what you want happen.

6) Working to get external power.

7) Holding on to old emotional baggage.

8) Finding doors closing in you face.

9) Fears coming up when you want to make positive changes.

10) Listening to and believing the ego propaganda.

11) The need to win at all costs.

12) Having expectations.

SIGNS THAT WE ARE GOING WITH THE FLOW

1) Trusting that there is a higher power directing your life and getting out of its way.

2) Coincidences, synchronicity and miracles.

3) Spotting the signposts.

4) Being at one with nature and the cycles of life.

5) Using and acting on intuition.

6) Accepting everything as being just what we need.

7) Living in the moment.

8) Valuing inner peace more than external success.

9) Having all our needs met in the perfect moment.

10) Eager anticipation for what lies ahead.

11) A willingness to ditch baggage whenever it presents itself.

TIPS FOR GOING WITH THE FLOW

1) Notice if and when you are in struggle and staying on the spot rather than moving forward in your life.

2) Look at what beliefs, goals or pressures from family or society you are buying into.

3) If you think about making changes, what fears does your ego feed you? e.g. You will be destitute, unable to support your family, you are running away from reality or you are going mad. REMEMBER, fears are

always an illusion and if you believe them they will keep you stuck.

4) **CHOOSE** to give up the struggle and **SURRENDER**. When you surrender, you simply decide to give up the fight and battle, you have not lost the war.

5) Hand over the controls of your life to your higher self to direct and guide where you go and what you do.

6) Going with the flow does not mean that you become passive, do nothing and wait for things to come to you. The more you put your energy out into the world, the quicker the right things will be able to present themselves. Do what you enjoy.

7) Actively look for signposts to point you in the right direction. Use your intuition to avoid any dead-end routes. This involves being awake and conscious.

8) Do not have any expectations or allow your ego to decide where you are going or what lies at the end of the journey.

9) Stay in the moment and wait to see what turns up to know where you are meant to be and what you are to do. Enjoy where you are in the meantime.

10) Use trust as the antidote to any fears or worries that may arise about the future.

11) If you find that you are actively doing things to go with the flow but are still feeling stuck, or that things are moving very slowly, then you will probably be carrying too much baggage with you on your journey. The focus for you will be in finding people or techniques to help you shift this baggage.

12) When you experience miracles, synchronicity or co-incidences, see these as confirmation that you are on track and with the flow.

13) Try not to fall back into struggle patterns or to struggle to go with the flow. Look to see how you may be

Principle No. 3
DON'T TAKE THINGS PERSONALLY

DON'T TAKE THINGS PERSONALLY

If this principle is adhered to, it can erase a huge amount of hurt and anger from our lives. Most of us go through life taking offence at a vast number of things. It may be the person who cuts us up on the motorway or the acquaintance who walks past us without saying hello or the boyfriend who does not ring when he says he will. Some of us have made taking it personally into an art form. We may even take on things that happen in another part of the world as being personal to us.

WE KNOW WHEN WE HAVE TAKEN SOMETHING PERSONALLY WHEN WE DO NOT FEEL GOOD.

We have got personally involved when we allow the words or actions of another person to adversely affect us. We come into this from a position of powerlessness because how we feel will be dependent on what others do or do not say. When we take our power back and learn not to take things personally, we are free to choose how we want to feel and behave.

We learn to take on other people's stuff at a very early age and many people do not grow out of it. When we are babies and small children, we think we are the centre of the universe and everything and everyone revolves around us. Consequently, whatever circumstances we experience in early childhood will feel as if they are down to us. This may be things like rowing parents, abandonment, poverty, illness, moods or depression. We build our belief systems about ourselves based on how we are treated and what happens in the first few years of life. For instance, a child

28

may think "I can't be a very worthwhile person because my Dad is always at work and doesn't want to spend time with me." An adult would of course see this differently and know that this was nothing to do with the child.

People who are particularly good at taking things personally are usually very sensitive. Sensitivity is an enormous gift if it is utilised properly. If it is misdirected it will seem to be a terrible curse. When we are sensitive, we experience everything through our feelings and we will often magnify them until they are out of all proportion to the situation we are in. Society does not tolerate sensitivity very well; it often perceives it as a defect in someone's character. It is most important that sensitive people learn this principle and put it into action in their lives. Feelings are the language of the soul and they are a vital ingredient needed to connect with our intuition and guidance that will make life easy and effective. When we are clogged up with negative emotion, we are unable to access the intuition as these feelings get in the way. To rectify this we need to release the old stored emotions and learn not to take on more by not taking things personally.

There are three main emotions that we tend to take on board when we take things personally. These are hurt, anger and guilt. We will look at these separately. Hurt is probably the biggest reaction we have to other people's words or actions. Much of our most destructive behaviour is created out of a misguided attempt to avoid hurt and pain. When we employ these protective mechanisms, we usually end up hurting ourselves and many others into the bargain. We may cut ourselves off and withdraw, in which case we shut out people who may love us and we hurt them by not being there or loving them. A common protection mechanism is to go on the defensive and attack others before they can hurt us. Once again this will backfire as people will either attack

29

us back or reject us for our aggression. Both of these will ultimately create hurt. There are still others who avoid hurt by constantly being on the go and active. You can never pin them down or even have a conversation as they are always in the middle of something else. The thinking behind this is that you cannot hit a moving target. However these people also lose out on love, intimacy, joy and many other benefits that life has to offer. Much of the hurt in the world is created by those who are set on avoiding feeling their own hurt. It is clear that this destructive cycle of behaviour needs to be broken and this can only be done by people choosing not to take the words and actions of others personally.

When we see that the destructive behaviour and words of others are simply a projection of their fear and hurt and actually nothing to do with us at all, we can decide not to take it on. Even when the attack appears to be personal, it is not. It is simply that the weapons the perpetrator uses are designed for maximum effect. When we get close to a person, they learn our insecurities and will use these to hurt us. When we are using this principle, we can substitute compassion for pain. The more vicious the attack, the more the person hurting us is in a state of fear or pain. If we saw a small child in this state, we would want to comfort or help them. Just because this small child is hidden behind the front of a fully grown person does not alter this.

HURT IS A CHOICE. It may seem as if hurt is an involuntary reaction but it is actually a habit or pattern that we get into. We react as we have acted before in similar situations. It is automatic and before we know it we are feeling sorry for ourselves and in pain. All we need to break this cycle is a degree of awareness. There is a moment between when the words or actions of the person take place and our hurt kicks in. In that moment we can make a choice. Do I choose to give this person my power and take offence at what they have just said or done? Or do I choose to see that this is not my problem and I do not have to suffer for something that has nothing to do with me? It takes a split second for that choice to be made, one option will create a negative situation and the other a positive one. Make sure that the choice is an active one and that we are not simply choosing to passively react as we have done before.

Anger is another emotion that results from taking things personally. Anger occurs when someone either does something we don't want them to or doesn't do something that we want them to. When we are angry, we have the need to put our anger onto someone. This will either be the person who triggered the anger or some other innocent person who happens to be around. We are often afraid to give our anger to the person involved. For instance, if our boss is giving us a hard time, we might take it out on a co-worker or subordinate or if we are angry with our partner, we may take it out on the children for a small transgression. We can see from this that our anger is not about the person we often dump it on. It is not personal to them and yet they will probably take it personally.

Some people who find it difficult to deal with hurt will often convert it to anger as this may seem more acceptable to them. However, while hurt only affects us, anger will have a destructive knock on effect on many people and this simply perpetuates the whole cycle. It is perhaps harder not to take on anger than hurt because it often has a very external application and is harder to disguise. It is a very tangible energy and we can often walk into a room and be aware of an angry atmosphere.

In reality we have no right to demand that a person does or does not do anything simply because we want them to.

This renders us powerless as we are unable to control the actions of others. It is never personal when someone makes us angry, it is simply that their chosen action or inaction does not happen to tally with what we want it to be. Intuition can play a useful part here. It will tell us who is likely or unlikely to let us down, it will help us to make choices that will limit any hassle or disappointment and it will help us to understand and accept people just as they are. All these things eliminate any need for anger and we have not given our power away.

Guilt is a very common reaction to taking things personally. This may even be the biggest reaction. It is hard to know this because guilt is completely internalised and there is often shame attached to the guilt and this prevents us from admitting to this feeling. Whenever we perceive ourselves to be guilty, we create punishment in our lives. This may be done in a variety of ways but all of them are detrimental to us. When people are manipulative or controlling, the weapon they often use is guilt. Controllers only have the power that we give to them and if we do not play their game, there is nothing that they can do.

GUILT IS ALWAYS A CHOICE. Most of the time we choose to feel guilty for things that have nothing whatsoever to do with us. For instance, our partner comes home in a bad mood, we may feel guilty and rack our brains for what we might have done to upset them. Moody people thrive on making other people guilty or responsible for their feelings. We live in a blame culture that looks to pin our misfortunes onto someone. We need to start taking responsibility for the things we create in the world. If we don't do this, not only do we not see the gift that situation provides but also we have to find someone else to be wrong or bad. Once again we project our own stuff onto other people.

Probably the main thing that we tend to take personally is the judgements and criticisms of others. There are some people in the world who consider it their duty to point out to all and sundry their faults, annoying habits and character defects. They view this as being beneficial to the recipient as they are clearly not aware of these things or they would have done something about it. We all know some very judgmental people and may even be one ourselves. We choose to focus on the faults and negatives within others and not on the good.

THE NEED IN OTHERS TO JUDGE OR CRITICISE US IS DUE TO A SENSE OF THEIR INADEQUACY AND NOT OURS.

If we judge others harshly, it is because we do not feel good about ourselves. We project our feelings about ourselves onto others in order to feel better about who we are. Our ego tells us that we are not as bad, as ugly, as stupid or as boring as they are. We may use this even more when we see people who seem to have or be more than us. They may feel like a threat to us, so we have to find all the things about them that are not up to standard and judge and criticise them. In a way this is a compliment to the person judged.

It is essential that we do not take on board the judgements and criticisms of others. We don't know the hidden agenda that is prompting the judgements and therefore the validity is in doubt. Constructive criticism is only constructive if the person involved has asked for it and respects the opinion of the person giving it.

We can put it into our heads that **WHAT OTHER PEOPLE THINK OF US IS NONE OF OUR BUSINESS.**

There are many of us that spend our lives worrying about what others think of us. We may put a great deal of time and thought into creating an image that we think will be acceptable to our friends and neighbours. This may be how we look, our behaviour or the things we have. The fact is that we have no idea how others think of us, so what we end up doing is projecting onto them our thoughts and beliefs about ourselves and believing that this is what they are thinking about us. This pattern of behaviour is born out of massive insecurity and is very destructive. We do not grow and experiment, we lose sight of who we truly are and we waste energy playing a role that is not us. People who do not care what others think are usually supremely confident. They might be quite unconventional but they do command the respect of others because they are real and do not see the need to conform.

The only opinion that should matter to us is our own. In learning not to take the judgements, thoughts and criticisms of others personally, we have to build our own self-esteem and learn not to judge ourselves. This is an ongoing process and we may have to catch ourselves each time we feel hurt, worried or devalued by our perception of the words or thoughts of others. Equally, we need to be aware of how much we judge others in both thought and word. Remember this is an indication of our inadequacy and low self-esteem. When we do this we lower ourselves and our vibration. There is a huge difference between an observation and a judgement. An observation will note something without putting a charge on it. A judgement is usually making someone less or wrong. We put a negative charge onto the observation and we may even enjoy bringing that person down to size.

Some people go through some very traumatic events in their life like rape, assault, burglary and muggings. Many victims do not manage to move through these traumas and they carry the fear and pain with them for the rest of their lives. These attacks will feel personal because they happened and we were invaded by them. We might wonder what is wrong with us that these things were aimed at us. Part of the healing will involve seeing that it was not personal but purely circumstantial. It was not anything to do with the victim but all about the perpetrator. We may also need to look for and find the gift in these situations.

DETACHMENT IS THE KEY TO NOT TAKING THINGS PERSONALLY.

This does not mean that we become shut off or hard in our approach to people and situations. Far from it. We are able to be more compassionate and understanding. Detachment means that we are not taking on other people's stuff. It is like taking a step backwards so that we can see the bigger picture without being embroiled in the emotion. We become aware that the words and actions of others is about them and not us. We can deflect any negativity away from us and not let it hurt us.

It may be more challenging to detach from those who are nearest and dearest to us. For instance, when we are living in the same house as a moody or difficult member of the family. We are set free when our feelings are not adversely affected by others. We may have to reclaim our power from this person before we detach. We may have got into the habit of putting so much focus on the other person, constantly tuning into their moods, looking for ways to pull them out of them or paving the way to prevent anything from upsetting them or setting them off. As soon as we detach, we make them responsible for their feelings and we give no energy to their negativity. We are able to be happy and content no matter what is going on around us.

Detaching does not mean that we are withdrawing our love. Indeed, we find it easier to give it when we are detached. Detachment does not allow others to take our energy or to drain us. Remember, what we put our energy into will expand. If this is other people's bad behaviour or negativity, then we are becoming part of the problem and not the solution.

Once we detach, we can begin to **CHOOSE** how we respond to other people. We can ignore them or we can choose to put light into the situation. This is done by seeing the funny side of things. Nothing lightens things more than laughter. This does not mean that we laugh at or ridicule a person. We simply look for an amusing slant on the situation. Believe it or not this can be done no matter how serious the circumstances. This is healthy and not disrespectful.

We have to take responsibility for ourselves alone. We make our choices based on who or what we want to be, experience, think and feel. We are not responsible for how other people feel or respond to us; that is their choice and need not affect us if we do not take it personally. If we have a reaction to other people's behaviour, then it is our responsibility to process and release this without blaming it on the person. They were merely the catalyst for showing us some unhealed damage from the past.

While we detach and don't take personally the negative words, thoughts and actions of others, we also need to not take personally the positive ones. It is very unhealthy to become dependant on compliments, praise or approval. When we feel good about ourselves, we do not need these. It is not a good situation to be put on a pedestal by anyone. They give us their power, which we don't want, and it is very lonely and precarious up there. We are constantly waiting for the moment when we come tumbling down in their eyes. We must realise that the positive beliefs from someone are also a projection. The most beneficial thing we can do is hold up the mirror to that person so that they can see the good in themselves. We empower and inspire them without taking on stuff that is not ours.

Freedom is the biggest gift we receive by learning not to take things personally. We are free from fear and we don't need to defend or protect ourselves from being hurt. We do not limit ourselves for fear that we will make others feel small. We can go into the most turbulent of situations untouched by the atmosphere and carrying our inner peace with us. We can open our hearts and not worry if someone will destroy our vulnerability. We can laugh our way through any difficult patches in our lives.

WAYS IN WHICH WE TAKE THINGS PERSONALLY

1) We feel hurt.
2) We feel angry.
3) We feel guilty.
4) We tailor our behaviour based on other people's expectations.
5) We worry about what others think of us.
6) We take on the feelings of others.
7) We take responsibility for the feelings and moods of others.
8) We see ourselves as victims.
9) We believe the judgements and criticisms of others.
10) We shut people out in case they hurt us.

11) We feel unworthy and allow people to confirm this.

12) We channel our sensitivity into the problem and not the solution.

TIPS FOR NOT TAKING THINGS PERSONALLY

1) Look at your patterns and see how you are in the habit of taking things personally.

2) How do you try and protect and defend yourself from being hurt?

3) Who are the people in your life that you find yourself being most affected by? Make a list.

4) Do these people hurt you, make you angry or guilty or do you take on their stuff or responsibility for their feelings and moods?

5) Use these people to practise on. Detach from them and **CHOOSE** not to be hurt, angry etc. Remember there is a moment after someone has said or done something to you before a reaction has set in. Use that moment to decide not to take their words or actions personally. Do not try to retaliate or defend. Disconnect from what is being said or done.

6) Remind yourself that everything others do or say or think is a projection of their feelings about themselves. Knowing this, it is easier not to take their stuff on board.

7) If people are controlling or manipulative, remember that it takes two people to play the game. If you **CHOOSE** not to play, there is nothing they can do.

8) Do not try to assume or worry about what others think of you. **WHAT OTHER PEOPLE THINK OF YOU IS NONE OF YOUR BUSINESS.** Even if people

do make judgements, detach from them.

9) Look at any events in your past that may have been traumatic. Are you carrying any baggage or residue from the trauma? Know that it was not personal, detach from the charge on the situation and allow yourself to move on.

10) Take responsibility for what you do, think and create but do not take responsibility for the feelings and moods of others.

11) Create a win for yourself. If you don't take things personally, you can be happy no matter what is going on for other people.

12) See the funny side of things. Choose to be amused rather than hurt by the words and actions of others.

Principle No. 4
FIND THE GIFT

FIND THE GIFT

We are living in very turbulent times and are bombarded on a daily basis with many things that are wrong in the world. The papers, television and films expose us to a diet of negativity. Unfortunately this is not balanced with the countless good things that happen daily. Consequently, we are becoming increasingly fearful, aggressive and insecure. We are not being given the positive role models needed to inspire us to get the most out of life.

With everything that happens there is an enormous gift attached. We are not taught how to look for and find these gifts. As a result we tend to get stuck in the negativity and are often unable to move forward. I will endeavour to show the most common gifts that we are given and can use beneficially in our lives. I believe that there is absolutely no situation that does not have some opportunity built in. In the more tragic circumstances this may be harder to find.

The greatest tragedy is when we do not find and use the gifts of a challenging situation. All the benefits that were available are wasted. However, it is possible to go back and reap the rewards with the advantage of hindsight. If we are willing to re-perceive aspects of our past, we can use the gifts that we failed to accept at the time. It is never too late.

Everything we experience in life is decided by how we CHOOSE to perceive things. It becomes our reality, not because it is true but because we give our power and energy to this belief and this will appear to manifest itself. We are very quick to form patterns. When we have perceived something once, when faced with a similar situation, we will tend to perceive it in the same way. Consequently we are programmed to think a certain way and we rarely question the validity of it.

In every moment we are either allying ourselves with either the ego or our true Divine selves. When we allow the ego to run us and perceive and judge what we are, it will always see us in a negative light. The ego will make us or someone else wrong or to blame for what has occurred. It will render us powerless victims who have no say in what we experience or even our successes. It will inject fear into even the most positive of circumstances thus diminishing them. It will tell us of our unworthiness, of our lack of deserving or that we are not good enough. It will judge others equally harshly. The ego will not be able to find the gift so we need to make sure that we do not put it in charge of doing so.

The Divine side of ourselves will only be able to see the good and positive in everything and therefore we can apply to it to help us to find the benefits. The inner Divine voice is very gentle and loving. It would not deny us the benefits of learning from our mistakes. The ego voice in contrast is very harsh and is always berating us for something. It is important to distinguish between these two and not be drawn into any ego propaganda. The inner Divine has the advantage of being able to see the big picture. It is able to see how something that is happening now is going to have a knock on effect that will create something good further down the line. We can often only see this with hindsight. For instance, if we had set our sights on a job that we knew we were perfect for and we did not get it, the ego will focus on the disappointment, rejection and fact that we are not good enough. The Divine would simply know that the job was not right for us and a better opportunity will present itself in a few weeks or months time. When we look back, we are relieved that we did not get the first job. The trick here is to know it at the time even though we have no concept of what lies in wait for us. This is where trust needs to be employed.

Death is one of the things that we as a society struggle with a great deal. Yet it is the one thing that absolutely everyone will have to deal with. The problem is that there is so much fear around death and also an uncertainty as to what lies beyond. It obviously helps to have a belief system that incorporates life after death and an understanding that it is only the physical body that leaves us. The essence of the person we loved remains and actually becomes more accessible to us. Many people tell me that they are able to have a better relationship with a deceased loved one than they had in life. However, if we are stuck in our grief or we try not to deal with it by keeping busy, we block any connection from reaching us. My personal belief is that death is the most wonderful thing that can happen to us. Our soul is liberated from a body which is a very difficult domicile for it. Birth is probably the hardest thing for the soul to endure, yet we celebrate the one and mourn the other. However a person dies, death will be a blessing. If the death has been painful or drawn out then it is a happy release from the pain and struggle. Equally, if the passing is quick and pain free, we can rejoice for that person that they were spared any prolonged pain and that the transition was made so easily.

When we experience a death in the family or our social circle, we are given the gift of tapping into all the pain of loss that we have experienced and not released in the past. If we take this opportunity, we can considerably lighten our load by releasing this heavy baggage. The death of Princess Diana is a good example of this. The outpouring of grief was not really for her, it was the unexpressed pain from all our pasts finding an expression. This was probably the biggest gift she could give to mankind.

Where death is hardest to deal with is when there are people who are dependent upon the deceased. This may be a husband or wife or a child who loses a parent. Without a doubt this is one of the most challenging circumstances we can face. We might be forced to find a level of independence that we would not otherwise have chosen. This can only be a benefit. If we are dependent, we give away our power and stunt our own personal growth.

We might all agree that the death of a child has got to be the most traumatic thing we could deal with. We might find death in an older person who has lived a life easier to accept. Many parents get stuck in this loss and find it hard to move on. Children here for a short time are often our greatest teachers, they fit a great deal into a small space. The ego will only dwell on the loss of the child. The Divine on the other hand will see the child as a gift in itself and instead of seeing the gift taken away, it will focus on what it came to bring. If a child dies, it was never part of the Divine plan for it to live into adulthood, so it is not losing out on anything. We often see how the life of a sick child brings the best out in so many people and good things result after the death of a child in its name.

The death of pets can also be a huge catalyst for good. Many people find it easier to love an animal than other humans. The depth of feeling may be every bit as strong as it may be for a child or partner. There is an inevitability that we will have to face the death of a pet. Our pets are so tuned into us that I often find that the timing of their deaths may be very significant for us. It may enable us to move on unencumbered or to make changes in our lives. The biggest gift that the death of a pet provides for us is once again the opportunity to access and release a huge amount of emotion. It is a great shame when we let this gift go by the wayside.

Sometimes the things that are seemingly the most difficult or challenging to deal with will offer the biggest gifts. These can come in the category of "Cosmic kicks up the bum." Anything that pulls us out of the rut or the treadmill is going to give us huge benefits. When we or someone we love has a life threatening illness, it forces us to reassess our lives and what is important. If we have put too much focus on material things these become meaningless when we are faced with mortality. Family, friends and our spiritual connection suddenly become our priorities. We may want to put everything in order, change our lifestyles and heal past wounds. People who have survived life threatening situations will often say that it was the best thing that happened to them because of all the changes in their life that it catalysed. The gift is always there.

When something is past its sell by date and we fail to notice this, something will often come along to make us see it. In the job field this may be redundancy, being fired, the company going into liquidation or forced early retirement. Sadly, many people do not recognise and reap the rewards of these situations. They get caught up in the rejection and feeling put on the scrap heap and may vegetate rather than look for the opportunities that they have been given.

The other area of life that comes into this category is relationships. The fact is that if a union is no longer right for one partner, it is not going to be right for both. Sometimes we get so caught up in the fantasy or trying to recreate the feelings we had when we first got together that we do not see that we have outgrown the relationship. There is usually one partner who becomes wise to this fact before the other. If we do not accept this natural conclusion, we get stuck in pain, anger, resentment and the need to punish our partners for putting us through this.

In reality the gift is that we are free to move on and experience other people who are on the same wavelength as us. If we can make this transition remaining friends and carrying forward the good times and growth that we have got from each other then we have no residue but only the gift.

The biggest "cosmic kick" that the world has seen in recent years is the tragedy of September the 11th. This has sent shock waves all around the world. It may seem hard to see the gifts involved in this situation but they are there. Firstly, it is a huge wake up call, it has shocked us out of our complacency and made us look at the big picture. It has reminded us of the importance of family, of not taking them for granted and living life to the full with the people we love while we have them. It has made us look inside for our answers and discover an inner world and a strength that offers so much more that the material world.

If we do not look for and find the gifts in the challenging situations in our lives, we often stay stuck within that occurrence and unable to move on. We may live in the hurt, guilt, fear or anger that have been created out of the experience. I have seen many people who carry this for the rest of their lives. Other areas of life count for nothing, it is as if the clock has stopped at the point of the difficulty. Often before we can see and appreciate the gift, we have to release and process the emotions and negative beliefs that have arisen out of the situation. This in itself is a gift. Everything that occurs has a lesson for us, even if it is to teach us not to do this thing again as it caused pain and hardship. Usually we learn more from our failures than our successes. The great inventors would agree with this. Everything that does not work brings us a step closer to the thing that does. If we let the ego loose in these situations, it will tell us that we are losers and that we may as well give up because we are useless and can't get anything right. Fortunately, the great people in history did not heed this propaganda.

Many people have had very difficult childhoods with absent or dysfunctional parents, abuse, poverty, deprivation and many other horrors. Some of the accounts I have heard in my practice make my toes curl. It can be hard to understand this and see the gift when these things happen to innocent children. However, I believe that we choose our childhoods and parents as the training ground to give us the experience and skills we need in order to do the life work we have come to do. For instance, who better to work towards stamping out bullying or abuse than someone who has been bullied or abused. They will have a better and deeper understanding of the issues and consequences involved than someone with no experience of the situation. Once we have this knowledge, we can let go of the aspects of our childhoods that make us feel powerless or a victim and only take forward the lessons and growth that we can put into practice in our adult lives.

Our greatest teachers in life are those who challenge us the most. We may hate them or resent them for causing us so much grief and hassle and we may completely miss what they are here to teach us because our feelings towards them are so strong. However, on a deeper level it is the souls who love us the most that would volunteer to help us learn our lessons. We lose sight of this truth when we are in the situations with them. This knowledge alone can completely transform any challenge or difficulty that we experience. We may need to take a moment to throw out all the human and ego baggage and connect with the soul behind it. When we have a sense of the love that is underlying, we are able to forgive the negativity and to thank them for the lessons they are providing. When we do this the relationship often heals and is conducted on a different level.

It is important to stress that finding the gift is not the same as being in denial. When we are in denial, we are afraid to face or deal with reality. We have to pretend that it either does not exist or we make it into something that we can cope with. There are some people who create a fluffy-bunny world for themselves and do not let the harsher realities enter into this world. When we do this, we stay stuck and do not learn the lessons that are being presented to us. Those who have turned denial into an art form are usually very frightened and they want to protect themselves from anyone who might invade and give them some unwanted home truths. As a result of this, they may be very controlling. The fact is that we have to see a problem for what it is before we can find a solution to it or reap the gifts and benefits it provides.

When we have expectations, it becomes very hard to find the gift. If we have set our sights on a particular out-come, we will always be disappointed if we do not receive this thing. When this occurs, it is usually because something better or more suitable has presented itself. It is very easy to miss this if we are fixated on something else. Expectations never serve us and it would be beneficial if we could banish them from our lives. Instead, we can instate expectancy. Expectancy says "I know good things are going to happen but I won't know what they are until they arrive." This puts us on our mettle to be looking for the gift instead of waiting for it to hit us over the head.

Whatever we put our energy into will expand. When we focus on bad things, this is all we get to experience. Equally, if we put our attention on the good bits, these become more prominent. This extends to people. Everyone is a good mixture of flaws and virtues. When we only see the faults, we tend to bring these to the forefront. If we choose to see good in people, we actually end up bringing out the best in them and this can be extremely empowering for everyone. Teachers who are able to do this are a very valuable commodity. We can all learn to do it. When we see a good quality in anyone, we can tell them. This will boost their confidence and self-esteem and may encourage them to focus on the good aspects of themselves and not the flaws.

One of the biggest gifts that people have to give us is a mirror by which we can see our own reflection. As a rule things we dislike or that irritate us about others will be aspects of our own personality that we do not like. This also applies in the positive. Traits that we admire in people are ones that we have. If we take advantage of this mirror, we can clear, release or learn to accept our own issues and not allow them to dominate our lives.

Gratitude is a very important concept. It is another way in which we may expand the positive by focusing and being thankful for what we have. We would not dream of being given a present and not saying thank you to the donor. It is therefore important to extend this gratitude to the universe for all the many gifts that are given to us. The more grateful we are the more we get. We know ourselves that if we have given a present to someone and we have received no response then we are not inclined to give any more. However, if we are shown how much pleasure our gift created and we are thanked, we want to create more pleasure by giving more. The Universe would have a similar response to this. The gratitude also acknowledges the receipt of the gift. Most of the gifts given are never received and therefore gratitude would not be forthcoming. There is nothing too small to be grateful for. The natural side benefit about gratitude is that it makes us feel good about ourselves.

COMMON GIFTS WE ARE GIVEN

1) An opportunity to release negative emotions like hurt, guilt, anger or fear. These can only be expressed when they come to the surface.

2) Space and time to attend to our own needs.

3) Wake up calls.

4) An opportunity to put ourselves back on track.

5) A signpost to guide us to the next thing.

6) A coincidence or miracle.

7) A mirror to see our patterns, issues and traits that may need healing.

8) The ability to use our experiences to help others.

9) The ability to appreciate what is important.

10) The chance to dissolve any negative residue.

11) A pat on the back for our achievements.

TIPS FOR FINDING THE GIFT

1) Acknowledge that there is a gift to be gained in virtually every situation. The bigger the issue, the larger the gift.

2) Avoid cosmic kicks up the bum by hearing messages and accepting the gift at an early stage and before something big has to happen to get your attention.

3) Attune to your intuition so that it may lead and guide you to any gifts and opportunities.

4) Have no expectations about the specifics of what may lie ahead. Simply have an expectancy that there will be good things and wait to see what turns up.

5) Open yourself to receive. Often we are better at giving

than receiving and can block good fortune from reaching us.

6) In order to find the gift, you may have to look for it first. You know when you get it because the whole charge of the situation you are in is different.

7) Always release any emotion that comes up and then acknowledge the benefits.

8) Look back at your past and childhood and acknowledge the challenges you were presented with as the training you have chosen in order to do the life work you have come to do.

9) Choose to see the gifts and good points in other people rather than just focusing on their faults. You expand what you put your energy into.

10) Look at the people who have challenged you the most or seemed like the biggest thorn in your side. What were the lessons that they were here to teach you? It may be acceptance, forgiveness or tolerance. Know that on a soul level these people love you very much and let this be the overriding factor you are left with.

11) Look at the mirror that people provide for you. Note the things you both like and dislike about them. These will be aspects of yourself. Accept the ones you like and set about changing the ones you don't. Any judgements you put onto others is simply a projection of your own dislike of yourself.

12) Learn to see the gifts in petty everyday occurrences as well as the bigger issues of life. It could be things like being in a traffic jam, bad weather, having arrangements messed about or cancelled, a power cut or any number of mundane things. If you train yourself to immediately look for the gift, nothing will ever phase you or cause any grief or annoyance.

Principle No. 5

DO UNTO OTHERS AS YOU WOULD BE DONE BY

DO UNTO OTHERS AS YOU WOULD BE DONE BY

This principle is hardly new or revolutionary. It has been around for about as long as man has and is featured in the teaching of most major religions. However, this has not meant that it has become part of human nature, far from it in fact. It is very hard to instil a mode of behaviour when all the examples around us show a very different way of being. Society teaches us how to be. We do what others do and often have to learn tactics in order to survive in the very damaged world that we have created. We may have learned that if we do not fight our corner, we will end up being short changed and others will get what is due to us.

There are two modes of behaviour that have superseded "Do as you would be done by." The first is "Give as good as you get" and the other is "Get them before they get you." These patterns simply perpetuate negative situations and create a huge amount of pain and misery. We have only to go to any play school or nursery school in the country to see both these modes of behaviour being played out on a daily basis. This shows us that the new actions have to be taught and learned many times over for it to become a natural part of our being.

One of our biggest motivational forces is trying not to get hurt either emotionally or physically. We look at ways of protecting ourselves from pain. However, most of the tactics we use to defend and protect ourselves will actually end up creating the very pain they are designed to avoid. Every time we defend or protect, we end up inviting attack. Both the "give as good as you get" and "get them before they get you" fall into this category. When someone hurts us and we immediately have the need to hurt them back, it does not stop there. The "tit for tat" will often escalate to the point where the initial bone of contention is lost and both parties become hell bent on hurting or scoring points over the other. Nobody ever wins these altercations and we end up putting up barriers or withdrawing deep inside.

The "get them before they get you" mentality is usually born out of a great deal of pain, usually in childhood where we were probably not equipped to deal with other people's damage. We believe that basically everyone is out to get us one way or another and therefore our only chance of survival is to get in first. However, the destruction created by this pattern of behaviour is huge. People will not want to get close to us, we are unpopular and will not get our needs met, this will create more hurt. It also gets us into "tit for tat" situations when we encounter other people determined to protect themselves or have a go at us because we are showing aggression. We often convert our pain into anger as this may seem to be a stronger stance to take than being a victim.

We will look at some of the areas of life that these two modes of behaviour affect most strongly. As I have already pointed out, small children can display these patterns from a very early age. It is most prevalent in two to three year olds where the angelic baby turns into a tyrannical monster. This is the age where the ego is developing. A child will hit out at its parents or other children who thwart it. This is the time to start teaching the principle. If little Johnny does not enjoy the experience of being hit over the head with a fire engine, then he should not whack Timmy in the face with a tractor. It is also important to stress that the child is not bad for having done it, it is simply the behaviour that is unacceptable. This lesson may need to be reinforced many times before it is learned.

54

These patterns emerge again in the school forum. Children have a capacity for enormous cruelty. They have the security of their peer group around them and will tend to aim their taunts at anyone who does not fit into the norm. This creates a two-tier system of insiders and outsiders. The truth is that those in the "in crowd" are feeling just as insecure, worthless and powerless as those who are not accepted. This pattern of behaviour is allowed to manifest in virtually every school, creating untold damage to thousands of children with sometimes catastrophic results. Once again, the "do unto others....." lesson needs to be taught as part of the school curriculum, not just as a theory but in practical ways. Tolerance of race, religion, looks and abnormalities does not seem to come naturally to us, therefore it must be instilled.

We can see these modes being used a great deal within the family, particularly with siblings. There is often a great deal of jealousy and rivalry in families. These patterns often carry on way past childhood. It is very difficult for parents always to be fair or not show any partiality. Some homes resemble a war zone with the adults trying to keep peace or limit bloodshed. Boundaries need to be very firmly set in these circumstances.

As adults the most prevalent area for the two destructive patterns to emerge is in relationships. This is one of the few scenarios where we allow ourselves to be vulnerable. When we fall in love, we open our inner selves to our partner. This can make us feel very exposed and we may fear being hurt by our other half. This often leads us to hurt them first in a warped attempt at protection. The resulting "tit for tat" usually ends up hurting both parties very badly. When we are in a relationship we know the insecurities, fears and weaknesses of our partner, we will usually use these to hurt them thus betraying any trust placed in us. For instance, if a man knows that his wife is unhappy with an aspect of her appearance, he can use this as a weapon to hurt her. Relationships have become about having our needs met. At the point where we do not feel that our needs are being met by our partner, we punish them by not meeting their needs. This creates a cycle of resentment and hurt that ultimately destroys the relationship. This is one area that "do as you would be done by" could break these very destructive patterns that the majority of relationships experience. This takes practice and discipline because it is very easy to go into attack or defence mode when we are feeling hurt. Some people take this to the extreme and want revenge for any perceived hurts. This may seem to give a few moments of satisfaction but will often attract even more pain in the long run.

The negative modes often play out at the highest levels in countries and governments. Virtually every war and the destruction and pain caused by them are created out of "get them before they get you" or "give as good as you get." The Middle East and Northern Ireland are two cases in point. The "tit for tat" killings have gone on for decades, never resolving the issues and simply creating endless fear, pain and aggression. How can we expect to teach our society to "do unto others..." if this hatred is perpetuated at the highest levels and sets an example that goes against the very religious teachings that we are meant to adhere to.

In politics the party system sets the two main contenders up against each other. Their job is to oppose anything that the other party proposes regardless of what their true beliefs are. This sets up a dynamic similar to sibling rivalry. They squabble all the time, telling tales on each other, trying to put the blame for everything that goes wrong onto the other one. Surely we all want the same things in life: good health, education, low crime, a healthy environment and a stable economy? It would make sense for everyone to work towards these goals, pooling energies, experiences and ideas rather than wasting time and energy fighting each other. Once again there are very few role models at the highest levels of government in the world to show us a better way.

Our whole path of evolution will be enhanced by our ability to learn and put into action "do as you would be done by." We are here to experience everything and then make choices based on that experience as to who we want to be and how we want our lives to be. When we have had things done to us, or done things to other people that do not make us feel good about ourselves, we have learned the important lesson that we do not want to repeat this experience or inflict anything onto other people that we did not like. It takes a level of awareness to achieve this. If we are not conscious, we carry on repeating the same patterns again and again. Each time we are in the same situation, we look at what we did last time and repeat it like a robot. The more highly evolved we become, the more deeply "do unto others..." becomes ingrained into our being. We don't even need to make a conscious choice, it is second nature.

We sometimes have to remove the expectation that if we treat others as we want to be treated that they should automatically return the favour. Very often they don't. This is not a personal affront to us. Other people are usually stuck in their own patterning and may not even be aware of what they are doing. It is very common in relationships to try and show our partner what we want from them by doing it for them. This will often backfire: they think we are doing it because we want to or enjoy it. They may not even want what we are giving them or take it for granted. Once again resentment will often result here. It is important that we do not get to a point where we lower our behaviour to match or fit in with those around us. When we set ourselves a standard, we cannot expect anyone other than ourselves to reach it. We may become a role model for others who follow our example but this is simply a side effect and not a demand.

There is a universal law that states that we get back what we put out. This is true but it does not necessarily come back from the same people that we give to. It may be given to us on a much higher or deeper level or in a completely different area of life.

We can see a complete absence of "do as you would be done by" within the arena of childhood abuse. The pattern that perpetuates this is so strong and it occurs in different races and cultures across the world. Where there has been sexual, physical or emotional abuse in childhood, many victims go on to abuse children, their own or others. This cycle of abuse affects a large percentage of people. We would think that if we know how awful it is to be abused, we would not want to inflict this on another human being. Sadly this does not seem to follow. Many men who have been abused will go on to abuse. This occurs less frequently in female victims who may be more likely to self-abuse rather than inflict it on others. This may be with cigarettes, alcohol, drugs, food or even self-mutilating.

"Doing unto others..." does not mean that we become a victim or doormat, who allows others to abuse us while trying to be understanding and forgiving. Far from it. We do not give away our power nor do we put up with unacceptable behaviour. This involves keeping strong boundaries and letting people know when they step over those boundaries. We do this without trying to punish them or pay them back for their behaviour to us and without getting defensive and attacking them. If people consistently step out of line, we may need to look at why we have them in our lives and is it time to let them go and move on. This may well be the message. If so, this can be done gently without having to hurt anyone's feelings.

The solution to breaking the destructive patterns lies with each individual. We can only do it for ourselves and it is the practical application of the theory that counts. If we preach a principle without living it, then the message does not get through. We teach through example and we do not even need to let anyone know how brilliant we are. If we live it, they get it. The thing that will reach other people is not a "holier than thou" attitude but letting others see the positive consequences of our actions. If we live this principle, we do not have to defend or protect ourselves. We can find a sense of inner peace, we can observe others struggling through life, but we are not dragged into it. We are not involved in constant power struggles, control or manipulation issues, for it takes two to play these games. We have such a simple premise by which to live. Would I want anyone to say, think or do this to me? If the answer is no then I choose not to do it to them. There are no great moral issues to wrestle with here and no rules that are created externally to have to live by.

At all times we can only do our best, this is the most we could possibly ask of ourselves. However, as we evolve and grow in wisdom and experience the potential for our best becomes greater. We often look back at what we have done in the past and feel guilty or ashamed and we may judge ourselves as a result. We did not have the same understanding available to us at the time as we do now. Every mistake we have made only serves to teach us and provide us with the opportunity to grow. We have to let go of the negative residue from our past and move forward with only the gifts that the experience had to offer. There is only now, and in each moment we are given the chance to be different and put into practice the theories that we have learned.

In putting this principle into action, we may need to make sure this is being done inside as well as in the outer world. Our ego is very quick to present us with judgements and criticism about other people. We may be nice to people to their faces but very judgmental about them in our minds. Our judgements are always a projection of how we feel about ourselves. If we do not feel good enough, we look for things in other people to make them less. An observation is different from a judgement. One is detached, the other has a negative charge attached to it. It is not enough to live "do as you would be done by", this could be extended to "think of others as you would like to be thought of."' This is an altogether tougher assignment but definitely one to work towards.

There is a concept of "right action" that we need to understand. Right action will only present itself in the moment. If we are tuned into our intuition, we will know exactly what it is. It comes from the depths of our innermost being. There are times when "right action" may conflict with society's or the churches' rules and this may set up doubt within us. There will be positive consequences to right action even if that is not immediately apparent at the time.

The ability to empathise can be a helpful quality in bringing in this principle. However, there are certain guidelines that need to be introduced. With empathy, we do not want to project all our feelings and sensitivities onto another person and think that they are thinking or feeling just as we would in the same situation. They may not. We then give them what we are actually crying out for ourselves. This is not healthy. Equally, when we empathise, we do not want to feel or take on other peoples' stuff onto ourselves. This simply doubles the problem and solves nothing. A degree of detachment is needed, we can tune into someone without feeling their stuff just as we can observe without judging.

If we use this level of detachment, we are also able to see what their needs are that might be different from our own. Where we might want to talk a problem through, another person might need the time and space to come to terms with a situation and someone demanding that they talk about it could be counterproductive. In "doing as we would be done by", we are not looking at the specifics but at the bigger picture. If we want to be respected, we give respect. If we want openness, warmth and love, then we give these things. If justice, truth and integrity are important, then we access these things within ourselves in our dealings with other people.

Another pitfall that we want to avoid is taking on or being responsible for fulfilling other people's needs because we are not getting our own needs met and would like it if someone came along and did so. This is what I call the rescuer. We find all sorts of lame ducks to try to rescue because we are desperate for someone to rescue us. The fact is that no one other than ourselves can actually rescue us. When this pattern occurs, we are in danger of burning ourselves out or becoming a doormat and we lay ourselves open to a great deal of pain. This does not serve anyone, least of all us. We are unable to fulfil others' needs, it is like trying to fill a bottomless pit. Instead, we can show others how to rescue themselves and to fulfil and meet their own needs.

This principle is a goal to work towards, it is not something that we will achieve overnight. We have to be gentle and understanding with ourselves. when we do not live up to the ideal.

TIPS FOR INCORPORATING "DO UNTO OTHERS AS YOU WOULD BE DONE BY" INTO YOUR LIFE

1) Make a decision to become part of the solution and not to perpetuate the problem by "giving as good as you get" or "getting them before they get you."

2) Look at areas of life or people in your life where these patterns play out. Do you try and hurt your partner, siblings, friends, work colleagues if you perceive that they have slighted or hurt you? Are you aggressive and protect yourself by having a go at people? Do you use any of these patterns of behaviour on strangers or anonymously for instance when you get behind the wheel of a car?

3) Ask yourself how it feels when you are at the end of someone else's hurtful or aggressive behaviour.

4) Look at where in your past these patterns have been created. Have they become so automatic that you are not even aware of what you are doing?

5) Make a list of things that are important to you in other people's behaviour towards you. i.e. respect, honesty, openness, kindness etc.

6) These are the qualities that you will want to give to yourself and others whether they require it or not.

7) Do not have the expectation that others will give you what you give them. They may be so damaged that

they only know how to project onto others how they have been treated.

8) **CHOOSE** not to be hurt, angry or defensive when others project their stuff onto you. It is their problem and not yours. It will only adversely affect you, if you give it the power to. Instead, use this as an indication of how much the other person is hurting. Send compassion to them instead of adding to the situation.

9) Become aware of the judgements you make about other people in your mind. Remember this is a projection of your dissatisfaction with yourself. Learn to be kinder to yourself, to accept you just as you are and this will then be able to be extended to others.

10) Do you look to others to lead the way? Choose to be the example that creates the ripple effect that can make a difference in the world.

11) Empathise with others without taking on their stuff or projecting your feelings and needs onto them.

12) Do your best but be gentle with yourself when you do not live up to the ideal. This is a process of evolution, it does not happen overnight.

Principle No. 6
CREATE YOUR OWN REALITY

CREATE YOUR OWN REALITY

We are the authors of our own lives. This may be a difficult concept to take on board because most of the time we seem to be powerless and victims of the whims of our culture, society, jobs, family and even location. It may appear as if we are dealt a random hand and are left to make the best of it. This is certainly the reality for the majority of people in the world because they have not been given to understand any other way.

We live on a planet of choice and we have been given the gift of free will and choice. We might not be aware of the extent to which this works for us because most of the time we are exercising passive choice and therefore we do not see how the things we are experiencing are created out of the choices we have made. The fact is that for everything we choose, there will be a consequence. Some of these are positive and some not so great. Once we can start to pair up the choices with consequences, we can decide what result we want and match this with the things that will create it. To do this we have to be awake and aware on every level. The more we evolve and grow, the quicker our choices will manifest. This can reach a point where it is almost simultaneous. For most people the gap between the choice and the manifestation will be so big that we do not associate the two things and therefore do not see how we created it. We need to acknowledge that by choosing to do nothing and make no conscious decision to create our reality, we are electing to give other people or situations the power to shape our lives. This is just as much our own creation as if we took charge and made our own choices.

The main way in which we create our reality is through our own perception. In every moment we are choosing how we want to perceive everything that is going on around us.

Two people experiencing the exact same situation may perceive it in totally different ways and consequently the reality will not be the same. If we allow our egos to perceive our circumstances, there will be a negative slant given to it. If we then give our power and energy to that perception, we create it as our reality. Our true selves would be more likely to find and see the gift or the funny side of things and make it a much more positive experience.

Most of the time we are not actively choosing how we want to perceive things, we are unconsciously opting to perceive them as we have done before in similar circumstances. The unconscious mind is like a computer that registers a program and stores it in its memory banks. When we are in a situation that mirrors the previous one, the whole program is resurrected and we repeat the pattern. How we perceived it, how we felt and what we did at the time. We spend our lives repeating and reinforcing our patterns. The more unconscious we are in our lives, the less aware we will be of our patterning. The fact is that we are still perceiving things in the same way as we did when we were a child or when we did not have the wisdom and experience to see it in its true light. We would not allow a child to tell us how to see life!

Breaking and releasing our destructive patterning is one of the most important things we can do. If we don't, we stay stuck in a rut that gets deeper and more difficult to get out of with every repetition. We will feel compelled to make the same choices even if we are able to see how destructive they are. Awareness is once again the first step. We may need to go back to the source of the pattern and look at how we chose to perceive the situation at the time. We can let this go and decide to see it in a more positive light. This new understanding can then be brought forward into our present day experience. When we become conscious and learn to live in the moment, we can see the potential in each second and choose to perceive everything as Divinely as possible. This may be a very tall order and it helps if our unconscious patterning is aligned with our current thinking because if we lapse into unconsciousness, we are not displaying any internal conflict of beliefs. Many patterns that we have are already positive and work well for us, we don't need to touch these. If it ain't broke, don't fix it!

There is another source of our patterning that may be harder to shake off. This is our family patterning. It is very common to see a repetition of circumstances passing down through the generations. Often it is the eldest child that is most like to carry this legacy. The effect may be diluted with later siblings. We often see patterns like suicides, illegitimacy, alcoholism or depression running in families and cycles of abuse are very well documented. We have to realise that the buck stops here and that we can break family patterns by choosing not to pass on a destructive legacy to future generations. We could even decide to start a few new beneficial patterns that could save the family. We can only break our patterns if we know that they are there. We can find out as much as we can about the family from as many different sources as possible as the perceptions will vary. This also helps us to understand why our parents are the way they are and what they went through. Many of us react against our parents and their patterns by going to the opposite extreme. This can be equally destructive and we may need to find the balance.

We may not be aware of the extent to which we choose and create our lives. Much of this is done by our higher selves before we are even born. We choose our parents, our race, religion, status and the very challenges that all of these things will give us. We also choose a potential or optimal life. To me this is the river of life that we are meant to flow with. This amazing life is already mapped out for us but because we have free choice and will, it is up to us to seek out and live our optimal lives. Sadly, very few people succeed in doing this and are more likely to stay stuck in the struggle, lack, powerlessness, fear and anger. If we are in touch with our higher selves, we are guided to the opportunities and miracles that will speed us on our way. However, the old saying comes into play here. You can lead a horse to water but you cannot make him drink. We can be led to the things that will create the best possible life for us but if we do not **CHOOSE** to act upon them, there is nothing that can be done. Contained within our potential or optimal lives is our life purpose and mission. There will be the opportunities for maximum growth and a great deal of fun, joy and laughter along the way.

One of the reasons why many of us do not embrace our optimal lives even when they are clearly presented to us is because there is a deep seated belief that we are not good enough or deserving of good things coming to us. I do not know anyone who has not bought into this universal belief on some level. It stops us from creating so many good things. This is clearly an illusion as we are all wonderful perfect children of the light in our essence. It is imperative that we all begin to dispel this illusion as it is keeping mankind stuck at a low level of evolution. The truth is that everything we experience in life is there to help us grow. If we do "bad" things or have "bad" things done to us, it is simply to give us the hands on experience to know if we want to repeat these things or not. We are not bad, wrong or deserving of punishment for having done these things and yet this is what we tend to believe. Not only are we good enough and deserving of all the bounty in the world, so is everyone else, no matter what they have done.

68

Some of the biggest blocks to our creating a positive reality are the myths that we are fed by society that we believe to be real and true. One of the biggest of these I would like to address because I think it is extremely destructive and causing untold misery is "The Fairy-tale syndrome." Most fairy-tales will follow a similar vein. The myth goes something like this. A beautiful girl who has had to face a great deal of adversity and pain in her young life gets rescued by Prince Charming who rides into her life on a white charger and saves her from poverty or difficult circumstances and they fall in love and live happily ever after. There are very few girls who have been exposed to this myth that have not bought into it. We are waiting for the ONE perfect man to come and rescue us. The fact is that he does not exist and many potentially good relationships are destroyed because they cannot live up to the very high expectations we have unrealistically created. When he turns out not to be Prince Charming, we are angry and resentful and may blame him for our disappointment. Many women spend a lifetime waiting for this person to show up, they may put the rest of their lives on hold so that they are not otherwise engaged when he arrives. This particular myth is fed and reinforced by fiction, films and the media. Multi-million pound industries are geared round this fantasy, so much so that it is hard not to be drawn into it. In my experience, in my practice when I put it to a client that none of this is real or true and should be released, I meet a huge wall of resistance. We do not want to give up this myth as it may have been the only thing that has sustained us or we have clung to in a turbulent life. I have to put it to these people that instead of holding onto an illusion that will not be real, would they rather create a guaranteed win for themselves to make all the things they want in a realistic and obtainable way. They tend to take some convincing.

The fact is that the only person who can rescue us is ourselves. The part of us that needs rescuing is in the child aspect of ourselves. We learn to bury and shut away the parts of ourselves that cannot function within the family or school environment. For instance, if there is a difficulty in the family, we may decide to be very good in order not to add to the problems. We may have to bury our enthusiasm, our exuberance, our feistiness, our spontaneity, getting our needs met, our playfulness, our anger and our pain. Some children go the other way and become aggressive, demanding and acting up all the time. They may have buried their sensitivity and gentleness, their laughter and play, their desire for knowledge and wisdom and many other qualities. In rescuing the child within, we can make it whole again by accessing and reuniting it with the parts of it that had to be suppressed or buried. We tend to look for others to give us these things and complete us particularly in relationships. This is a tall order and very rarely works. We may even find that they emphasise our lack rather than remove it. Many people are attracted to those who display the qualities that they feel they are lacking.

People who have a need to rescue, care for or fix other people are usually the ones most wanting to be rescued themselves. The hope is that people will follow their example and rescue them right back. However, these people will appear to be very strong and capable on the outside and will give no hint as to what they are needing or wanting. These people will also tend to attract and be attracted to people who are needy rather than strong and supportive.

Many of us felt we had to sacrifice ourselves in childhood in order to save one or more members of the family. This is done with good intentions but will tend to carry on into adulthood with not very positive results. Some children deflect emotions onto themselves, this may be to stop parents arguing or to take the attention off a sibling that might be struggling. If we have a pattern of being the scapegoat, this may show itself in all areas of life. We may give up things so that others may have more or take the blame for things that have nothing to do with us. There are many modes of sacrifice that will not be very obvious to the family or outside observers. Patterns of sacrifice need to be dispelled at source as they will block us from creating an optimal life.

There is a clear formula for creating our own reality. This is thought, word and action. We start off with an idea or inspiration. From this we put it into a cohesive form in words. This may be the spoken or written word. It is turning the pure thought energy into something more tangible. At this point we may need some intuitive guidance as to how to bring this into reality. This will always involve some action. This is our intention and commitment to the situation. The universe is then able to support us if this fits into the Divine plan. Many people have lots of inspiration and they might get as far as putting it into words but they often fall at the final hurdle because the ego will get in on the act and sabotage the process. It will present us with our fears, all the reasons why this would be stupid or unworkable. It takes courage to override the ego. When or whether an idea will manifest will also depend on the degree of inner power and energy that we invest in it. The more energy we put out, the more that will be able to come back to us.

There is a huge amount of peer pressure put on us to be like everybody else. Society tells us how we should dress, what things we should buy and how our lives should be. If we do not fit into the norm, we are given the impression that we are not acceptable. My mother always used to say "just because others stick their head in the fire, doesn't mean that you have to." This is exactly what we do in order to fit in.

This is a huge stumbling block to creating our own reality. We have all been creating the reality that everyone else has even if it is limiting, in a state of lack, struggle and suffering. It takes a very brave person to create a different reality from those around them. We will be seen to be not like everyone else. It may feel as if we have put our heads above the parapet and are going to be shot down for daring to go against the norm. This will only be our reality if we CHOOSE to create it or perceive it as such. The fact is that we can be spearheading a new trend and in the meantime we can be reaping the unlimited rewards.

It is not just our peer group who are not keen on our being different or making changes, we ourselves are often the stumbling block. We will often opt for what is familiar and tried and tested even when we know that the outcome will be negative or destructive. We do not like to leave our comfort zones for new uncharted territory, even if there is a promise of great treasure at the end of it. We can test ourselves by pushing out the self imposed boundaries and grow in confidence and not be afraid of the unknown. Things that we have not done before will always create a bit of fear but once we have the courage to do them, it becomes easy and frees us up to try new things. This may be something like singing or talking in public or doing a fire walk or a parachute jump. This gives us much more scope for how we live our lives. The possibilities become endless.

TIPS FOR CREATING YOUR OWN REALITY

1) Look at the reality you have already created in your life. Make a list of the aspects of it that do not reflect who you want to be.

2) Become aware of the many patterns that are playing out in your life. Look at your patterns in relationships, in friendships, in the work place and in domestic issues. Some of these patterns will work for you while others won't.

3) Observe your family patterns. What legacies have been handed down through the generations. Ask questions about the family and ancestors. Build as full a picture as you can. Notice if you have taken on any family patterns. If so, know that you can **CHOOSE** to be different.

4) Remind yourself that how you perceive a situation is what it becomes. With this knowledge in mind, actively choose how you want to perceive every episode that you encounter each day instead of passively choosing to perceive it as you have in the past.

5) What myths do you buy into? If you are a female, do you believe in fairy-tales and are you waiting for Prince Charming to rescue you? Notice how these myths may have coloured and affected your life.

6) You can create what you want by making manifest your ideas and inspiration. Check first that these things are compatible with your Divine plan or you will create struggle. Take the thought or inspiration and put it into a cohesive, tangible form in words. Check with your intuition for the best way to put this

into action. Do not let your ego talk you out of it. Try not to leave too long a gap before you put it into action or you will have lost momentum and may find it hard to regain the same enthusiasm.

7) Do you feel deserving or good enough to create a wonderful reality for yourself? If not, you may need to look at the issues that have contributed to this and do some healing of the inner child.

8) Do you try to fit into the norm? Do you have to have or do things simply because other people do? Do you worry about what other people think of you. What would it feel like to dare to be different? What changes would you like to make? Start to do this now. You may become a trend setter rather than a sheep.

9) Notice what your comfort zones are. Does this limit you in your life? Do you envy people who are willing to push back the barriers? Start to do little things that broaden your horizons. Go to new places, try adventurous foods or join a club.

10) Be aware that your higher self has mapped out an optimal life for you. Tune into what this might be and remove patterns, beliefs and behaviour that is not compatible with this life.

THE PROCESS FOR REMOVING UNWORKABLE PATTERNS

When a pattern is identified, you may need to go back to the source in order to release it. It may also be necessary to remove some of the more predominant repetitions of it along the way, this is a bit like peeling back the layers of an onion until you reach the core.

1) Choose a pattern that you have become aware of that is not beneficial to you.

2) Look at all the different aspects of the pattern. Who or what do you attract to you? How do you react to the person or situations? What emotions come up within this pattern? What stages do you go through within the pattern? How does it normally conclude? Does this pattern occur in one particular area like in relationships or at work or right across the board?

3) Look at and make a list of the major repetitions of this pattern, starting with the most recent. Each of these will represent one layer of the onion.

4) The source of this pattern will probably be in childhood and often in the first five years of life. This may not be anything that would appear too big or life shattering to an adult but to a child it will seem much more significant. You may be aware of a family dynamic or incident that might have created the issue. If you are not aware of the source then you will be able to get the information from the unconscious mind during the clearing process. Don't try too hard to think it on a conscious level as this may block you. Relax and let the information present itself.

5) Take some time and space to do the process. Sit comfortably and close your eyes. Take some deep breaths to relax the body and still the mind. You are working with the unconscious mind to remove the destructive patterning. Focus on how the pattern has showed itself in its most recent incarnation. See all the players in it and really get in touch with it. See a metaphorical bonfire in front of you. Everything you want to release can go into the bonfire. Focus on the emotions involved in this. Is there anger, hurt, fear or guilt? Breathe out the emotions and see boxes of them

being thrown into the fire. What beliefs have been created in this pattern? Command the unconscious mind to delete and erase them. Choose to let the whole pattern go. You may want to press an eject button which brings a video of the pattern to the surface. Throw the tape into the flames. Unpeel the layer of the onion and throw it in the fire, symbolically letting go of the pattern. You now want to heal any aspects of this pattern. If you have given your power away to someone, you can take it back from them. See the power coming back to you in golden globules of power and energy. You may need to look for and find the gift the situation was there to give you. You might have taken things personally that were nothing to do with you. If so, detach from them. You might also have gone into a payback mode and wanted to punish someone for their part in the issue. If so, let go and forgive them. Visualise a whole new way of being and reacting in this pattern. Push this new video down into the unconscious mind and memory banks to replace the old pattern.

6) Repeat this process for each layer of the pattern that you have identified, going right back to the core.

7) If you do not know the source of the pattern. Relax and ask the unconscious mind questions.

a) Identify your age. Are you under 10, under 5, under 4. etc.

b) Was this a specific incident that happened or an ongoing situation.

c) Ask who the other players in the cycle are. e.g. parents, siblings, teachers, family members or friends.

d) If a specific incident is indicated, was it at home or somewhere else?

c) Was it during the day or night?

f) In what room or place did it occur?

g) Was it something said or done to you or something you witnessed?

h) What happened?

i) How did this make you feel at the time?

j) What beliefs did you take on from this?

8) Repeat the release and healing as with the other layers.

9) Bring the new pattern forward in time into this present day.

10) Any time you see yourself going into a similar situation. CHOOSE to react and perceive it differently.

THE PROCESS FOR RESCUING THE INNER CHILD

This process applies whether you are male or female. Even though the Cinderella complex is geared towards women, there is an equivalent within men.

1) Acknowledge that the only person who can rescue you is you. Be willing to give up the myths and fairy-tales that make you powerless or a victim.

2) Take some time and space for yourself. Sit comfortably and take some deep breaths to relax the body and still the mind.

3) Look at the aspects of yourself that have been buried. These will be the qualities that you perceive to be lacking in your life. It may be confidence, courage, creativity, fun, laughter, adventurousness, abundance, sensuality, spontaneity or connection with feelings.

These may be things that you admire and are attracted to in others.

4) How did you sacrifice yourself to save one or more members of your family? What has the effect of this been? Are you still doing this in some way?

5) Ask your unconscious mind how old you were when you either sacrificed yourself or buried aspects of your inner child.

6) Symbolically, where has this part of you been put? Is it in a tower, a locked room, a cupboard, a box or a trunk?

7) See you the wise, nurturing adult going to rescue the little one. Break down any barriers standing in your way. Pick up the little child and carry it out into bright sunlight. Let the light have a wonderful affect of awakening the true child. See it opening up like a bud going into bloom. See all the wonderful qualities in this child being activated and merge it with the aspects of the child that remained. See it becoming whole and complete. Tell the child that you love it and will be there to guide, nurture and help it. Let it know that it is safe and secure because you are in control of its environment. Build up a relationship of trust so that it knows that it can be itself. Watch as this amazing personality emerges, full of light and life and embracing the wonder of living. Tell the child how clever, beautiful, funny and fantastic it is. Let it know how proud of it you are.

8) Anchor this wonderful child inside your heart. Know that this is an integral part of you that can contribute a huge amount to your life.

9) Do not neglect your inner child. Nurture it when it feels frightened or insecure. Take it out to play and

Principle No. 7

USE YOUR INTUITION

USE YOUR INTUITION

Intuition is a part of our natural being. It is present in every single person in equal measure. Having said this, comparatively few people use it to the full and many people are completely unaware of its existence.

Ideally intuition would come to us as easily as breathing: we would not need to give it a second thought, it would just be there in every moment. However, as intuitive asthmatics we have to learn to open up the "air waves" and connect with this very powerful gift.

As with most things in life, the process we need to go through to connect with our intuition is not one of creating or looking for it but removing all the things that are in the way of our discovering it within us. It is a releasing and clearing process that automatically results in accessing and using our intuition on a constant basis.

Under the umbrella of intuition many different areas can be covered. To me the intuition is merely the means we have to link into unseen energy vibrations. We can link in with our higher selves and receive the benefit of its guidance and wisdom. We can link in with other beings whether they be guides or helpers or dead loved ones. We can link in with the thoughts, feelings and vibrations of other humans, even those who live thousands of miles away and we can link into nature and the natural world all around us. The intuition is the means within us to achieve these ends, it is not the source of them. Sensitivity is viewed by our modern society as undesirable. Many parents try to eradicate signs of it within their children and most particularly boys. However, our sensitivity is an essential part of the intuitive process. Without the ability to get in touch with our feelings, we may find it difficult to access our intuition. Intuition is often called the sixth sense. Sensitivity in childhood may seem to be more of a curse than a gift. Without understanding what is going on around us, we pick up on the thoughts, feelings and dramas of our family and friends. Many of us are also emotional sponges and we absorb the feelings that we encounter in others. We do not have the experience or means to process them or to distinguish them from our own. When this occurs many children find that the only way to survive these painful and intense feelings is to shut down the emotions. While this may alleviate the pain, it also shuts out joy, love and our access to intuition.

There are many things that may get in the way of our using or getting a clear message from our intuition. The biggest of these is probably the ego. The ego is very confusing because it does not always keep to the same story. Sometimes it will put us or others down for one thing and then at a later date the opposite behaviour will attract censure.

The ego will only ever feed us thoughts and feelings that have at some point in our lives been true for us. If we have experienced failure, it may tell us that we are useless and bound to fail again so there is no point in aiming for any degree of success, we will only be rejected and disappointed. Most of us listen to and believe the ego voice and consequently live lives of fear and limitation. The ego will often tell us that it is looking after us and protecting us from the pitfalls of life.

The ego has a very important and positive role to play in our lives. It is there to show us all the things that are unhealed within the unconscious mind and memory banks. If we are aware of this and process every negative aspect that does not serve us in who we want to be, we can eliminate these from our lives. Without the ego to bring these things to our attention, they would remain buried but

81

lowering our energy vibration.

One of the main ways in which the ego sabotages our intuitive experience is that it disguises itself as the intuition. It tells us in no uncertain terms that this is what our spirit or higher selves have in mind for us. It sends us on wild goose chases and it tells us that we are so much more Divine than anyone else and therefore we should tell them what to do and how to lead their lives. True Divinity is a state of being and not doing. It is a presence and not a pretence and anyone with a degree of intuition will pick up on this. One of the hardest parts of our development is distinguishing the ego voice from the intuitive Divine voice.

The first thing to be aware of is that the ego comes through thoughts while we connect with intuition through feelings. The solar plexus is the feeling centre and sadly we still have a great deal to learn about this amazing part of us. I call it the feeling brain and indeed it has been found that there is some brain tissue in this region. It is a vast network of nerves that resemble the rays of the sun, hence the name. These nerves are not feeding any organs. I think so little is understood because feelings are intangible, invisible and hard to monitor or analyse scientifically.

We often call intuition a "gut feeling" and indeed when my inner self is trying to get a message through, I can feel very strong sensations within the solar plexus.

It is essential that we learn to separate our thinking minds from our feeling ones, so that we can make sure that the messages we are receiving have not become tainted by the ego and its agenda. One clue that we have about the source of the information is the words we use. If we start a sentence with "I think...", this probably comes from the mind. If we find ourselves saying "I feel..." it will be coming from the gut. In fact I often hear people say "I don't know how I know this but..." Intuition does not need logical explanations or reasoning in order to know something. Nor does it need proof that this knowing is true before acting upon it.

Another way in which we can work out if a message is coming from the ego or the intuition is by the content. Intuition is gentle and loving, it does not want to put any struggle or difficulty into our lives. It is there to guide and help us through. The intuition will often reassure us that even challenging situations are a positive in our lives. It teaches us to go with the flow and allow the magic of our lives to unfold in miraculous ways. it would warn us against getting into situations that would create unnecessary pain or fear at the same time as trying to extricate us when we do.

The advice the intuition gives us will usually make us feel good while the, ego creates quite the opposite feeling. We always know when the right decision has been made, no matter how illogical. We feel as if a weight has been lifted off our shoulders and there may be feelings of excitement and anticipation. These are the opposite of fear and worry that are the domain of the ego.

The next most common block to our intuition lies within the feelings. FEELINGS ARE THE LANGUAGE OF THE SOUL. They are the means by which we connect with the inner self. However, feelings cover a wide variety of emotions, love and fear, anger and passion, joy and pain, shame, guilt, envy and many more. When we are holding onto many negative feelings and we store them inside, we are blocked from connecting with the intuition.

Ideally our emotions are very fluid and they flow. We feel something and then we express it from the body leaving us free to experience the next emotion. However, when we do not process, express or allow our feelings to flow out, we have to suppress them within the body.

The solar plexus as well as being the intuitive communication centre also becomes the junk room for unexpressed negative feelings like fear, anger, hurt and guilt. If we are holding onto a great deal of old emotions, this area becomes a no go zone. We do not dare connect with our intuition for fear of tapping into anger or pain that we have done our best to avoid. This whole understanding would be unconscious rather than conscious. We go through life trying to protect ourselves from feeling these emotions. Notice how often we cover our solar plexus with our arms, clothes or even excess weight, when we are in situations that make us feel vulnerable.

It is essential if we are going to work with our intuition that we clear out the old emotions and create a space to allow good communication to come through. This process can be gradual and need not be remotely traumatic. Just as we would clear out an attic or junk room, systematically unpacking each box and chucking out everything we do not want to keep, we let out the emotions that do not serve us or block our development.

Once we have put out the intention to clear out our emotional baggage, we can relax and allow life to show us which bag to clear next. Every time a button is pushed and anger, fear or guilt come to the surface, we are being given an opportunity to let them go. This means expelling them from the body and not pushing them back down again. If we welcome each trigger and the resulting feelings, the process can be gentle and effortless.

Many people have completely disconnected from their emotions. Sadly, this is often praised in our society: the stiff upper lip; not giving in to the weakness of emotion. When we detach from our own feelings, we also become unaware of other peoples' sensitivity and we may well trample over them, creating a great deal of pain in the process. When we sever the connection with feelings, we also cut off the link with the intuition. In these cases, it would be necessary to go back and reconnect at the point in the unconscious where the trauma took place, clearing out the emotions at the same time.

The major bonus that occurs with clearing out and processing the emotions is that we feel good. We allow the gentle flow of positive emotions to occur because the blockage is no longer there from the suppressed negative feelings. These good feelings allow us to tune into the rhythm and flow of nature all around us.

THE PROCESS FOR DEVELOPING INTUITION

CREATE A RELATIONSHIP WITH THE INNER SELF- Ideally we want to reach a point where in every moment we are CO-creating our lives with the Divine aspect of us within. Our intuition is the means by which we connect with it. We want to have a friendship or relationship with this amazing being that we truly are. We therefore need to personalise it and treat it as we would a wonderful loving friend. It may help to give it a name and to bring it into every part of our lives, from what we have to eat to what route to take on a journey. Nothing is too mundane for it to be bothered with. We can also share all the good things of life with it. If we wake up and it is a beautiful day, we can take a moment to enjoy it with the inner self. We can also laugh and joke with it as we would a friend. It may be surprising what a sense of humour our Divine selves have.

This building of a relationship is a gradual and ongoing process but it serves to strengthen the links we have with the Divine and therefore the quality of wisdom and guidance that is available to us.

ASKING - It is essential that we are clear about what we are asking for from the intuition. If the questions are too fuzzy or too broad, the answers will also be and we may miss them. We only get back what we put out. For instance, instead of asking what our life purpose is, we may ask to be shown the next step towards achieving it. When we break things down to bite size pieces, we can begin to get our teeth into the answers we receive.

Everything in life is energy and asking is one form of putting our energy out. The reply is the flow of that energy returning. If we just sit around and wait for information to come through, we may be sadly disappointed.

It is also important not to ask too many things at the same time as this confuses the issue and often results in no clear reply. Also if we make ourselves very busy and active when asking for what we want, we may well miss any answer that comes.

BREATHING - Breath is one of the most important components in connecting with our intuition. It is our link to the communication centre. It is what enables us to pick up the inner phone.

The breath is one of main carriers of energy and it takes what we are asking to the solar plexus. With the connection to intuition, the breath has a double role to play. First of all, it removes the focus from the mind and thoughts. Long, slow, deep breaths will also relax the brain waves. If we put our attention onto the breath, we are linking into the feeling brain and not the thinking one. The breath is also the means by which the question and intention is taken to where it needs to go.

Many people breathe very shallowly with only the upper chest moving. The breath has got to reach the solar plexus or the connection will not take place. It may therefore be necessary to do some work on deepening the breath. The solar plexus will move if the breath has reached it.

TUNING IN - Tuning in is an essential aspect of this process. We have to be on the same wavelength as the source of information or guidance or we will not receive what we need. This part of the process becomes easier with practice, it may take a few misses before we hit the right wavelength.

We all have examples of amazing coincidences with people that we are close to and with whom we share similar attitudes and feelings. We think of them and they ring or we say or think exactly the same thing at the same time. We are tuned into the same wavelength as they are and consequently communicate through unseen channels. This will happen automatically and without conscious effort on our part.

We have the ability to tune our energy into many different wavelengths but this does take our conscious participation. We have to get our own thoughts and persona out of the way. We also need to focus and concentrate our energy where we want it to go. It may be to another person, to Universal wisdom, to our own higher selves or to guides and loved ones on the higher realms.

I find that when I tune in, the focus and concentration are such that world war three could break out around me and I would not notice. This concentration is easier to achieve on other people's behalf than on my own as my ego is keen to butt in on anything to do with me.

There is always going to be some fine tuning to be done as we get more experienced in this process. If there does not seem to be any connection made, there may be more clearing needed to raise our own personal wavelength and vibration to a point where we can link in with others.

RECEIVING THE ANSWERS - The answers or the help and guidance we receive from the intuition comes in so many different guises that we need to be aware in order not to miss them.

Sometimes these come directly through our senses. If we are visual, we may receive pictures the interpretation of which may need some practice. Some people hear messages as if a voice were speaking to them. However, the majority of people sense the reply, it is an impression or imprint that the inner self picks up. This is often very subtle and may be missed by those who are not aware.

Much of the communication we receive comes to us indirectly. We may pick up a book and open it at a page containing the reply. A program on TV or the radio may do it or we bump into a friend who supplies the information. We see an advert in a paper or we are given a signpost by nature or our environment. It maybe a case of amassing clues from various sources and putting them together to form a big picture.

Within this part of the process, we need to view it with a degree of detachment. If we already think we know the answer to what we are asking and are simply looking for confirmation, we may manipulate the reply we receive to fit in with these assumptions.

Have no expectations and make no guesses as these are created by the ego and will distort any truths we are given.

TRANSLATING THE REPLY - There can often be a great deal of distortion from the receiving of a message or impression to putting it into a more tangible form. Once the ego gets hold of it, doubts begin to set in. Where did this come from? How do we know it is true? We'll look very stupid to other people if we believe something so tenuous.

The ego will also try to bring in logic and analysis, we may analyse so much that we lose sight of the original message. It will begin to debate the pros and cons of this message, it may even bring up many fears around this area, leaving us feeling so bad that we dismiss the guidance.

We all have an built-in truth monitor and it is important that we employ this as soon as any communication is received. Once the truth is established, we do not need to get into any debate with the ego. We put the message clearly into words, ready to go to the next phase of the process.

Some people find it helpful to write down what they receive as soon as possible before the ego has a chance to put the kibosh on it.

PUTTING IT INTO ACTION - Without this phase of the process, all would be for nothing. It is only when we act upon any communication that we are able to show that we have no doubts about its validity.

The longer we delay this action, the harder it will be to implement. The moment might have passed and we missed it. Failure to act upon information received, in effect blocks our flow and the energy is wasted.

There are many people who receive wonderful inspiration from unseen sources and yet are unable to act upon any of it. The ego once again is the saboteur here. It gives many reasons why we should not do these things and they will seem to be very plausible. If we believe them then the magic of our information is lost to us.

TRUST - Trust is essential in the intuitive process. First we have to trust that there its a higher power that has our best interests at heart and who we can connect with and receive guidance from. We then need to trust the information we receive, without demanding further proof or verification. Finally, we need to trust our ability to carry out any instructions that we are given.

Doubt is a very destructive force and if it is allowed to enter into the equation it will destroy all trust. With doubt we will find it very difficult to move forward in our lives, we will be revisiting the same territory time and again, stuck in a huge rut that we feel powerless to get out of.

TIPS FOR BRINGING IN INTUITION

1) Take some time to formulate a clear and specific request.

2) Know what you are asking for. e.g. advice, reassurance, support, a miracle!!

3) Clear space in a busy life to ask for what you need and leave room for the reply if it is meant to be instantaneous.

4) BEWARE of telling the intuition what it is you expect from it. This may not be for your highest good and will be met with a blank.

5) Take time to "be" and connect with nature as this will often provide a great deal of the energy needed.

6) Use the breath to keep a sense of focus.

7) Feel as if you are fine tuning a radio or TV aerial to get a clear picture or sound.

8) Do not allow thoughts or distractions to cut the link.

9) Focus attention away from the ego and self.

10) Keep sending out the intention to receive a reply and tune in.

11) Keep conscious and aware, in order to pick up the communication.

12) Work on honing your strongest sense, this will be your main form of receptor.

13) Look out for the signs and clues provided in the outside world.

14) Remain detached and have no expectations or preconceived ideas.

15) Put a plan of action together as soon as communication is received.

16) Ask to be shown the right time to implement this action.

17) Do not give energy to any of the ego's fears.

SYNOPSIS

1) Clear and release negative emotions that block the flow of feelings that connect with intuition.

2) Learn to identify the loving intuitive voice within.

3) Build a relationship with your higher self.

4) Be clear about what you are asking.

5) Use the breath to connect with the solar plexus and feelings and detach from the ego mind.

6) Focus and tune into the correct wavelength.

7) **SURRENDER!** Allow the guidance to come to you gently. **DO NOT TRY TOO HARD OR THIS WILL ENGAGE THE MIND.**

8) Be awake and aware of answers when they come.

9) Ask yourself if they feel right.

10) Put information received through your inner truth monitor.

11) Put the communication into a tangible form in words.

12) Act upon these words in the right place and time.

13) **TRUST, TRUST, TRUST.**

NOTE. This is a practice that will be honed with time and experience. Do not expect to be Nostradamus straight away.

Principle No. 8
BE YOUR AUTHENTIC SELF

BE YOUR AUTHENTIC SELF

In a way our whole journey on Earth is about finding our way back to who we truly are. This may sound strange but our real identities have become buried under a great deal of rubbish that many fear is who they are. Most of our growth involves sorting the wheat from the chaff and discarding the bits that do not tally with our true authentic selves.

The fact is that in reality we are ALL loved and loving, powerful beyond measure, abundant, wise, creative, joyful, beautiful, compassionate, peaceful, understanding and completely at one with everything. This is our true Divine state that we perhaps only get glimpses of from time to time. Everything else that we believe or perceive is part of a massive illusion that virtually the whole world has bought into and is therefore creating on a daily basis. It will only take a small percentage of people to wake up and to live their true authentic selves to start a new revolution that will completely transform our existence. We can decide whether we want to be part of the advance party that does the path-finding and paving the way for others to follow behind or to stay like everyone else and to conform. It has to be said that the rewards for choosing to be a maverick are enormous and as we begin to reap these with every step we take, it becomes the encouragement to keep going.

In finding our way back to our authentic selves, there is a great deal of clearing that needs to be done along the way. We want to eliminate what I call the "veils of illusion." Some of these are emotions like anger, hurt, or guilt. Some are belief systems that keep us stuck in negative thinking. Some are deep seated patterns that have been repeated so many times that they have become part of us and our life experience. We will always be shown our illusions. This will

94

either be because someone or something comes along and pushes a button that brings these things to the surface and therefore to our attention, or our issues will be reflected back to us by the people we attract into our lives. For instance, if we notice that there are a great many angry people around us, this may be an indication of the amount of anger that we have inside that we might not be comfortable with dealing with. I tend to find that once the issue is cleared, we do not tend to attract or notice the mirror image.

Every time an illusion is shown to us we have the choice as to whether we release it and remove the negativity or reinforce it by repeating old patterns and adding another veil to the pile. Most of the time we unconsciously choose to do the latter because we are not aware of how powerful we are and that we can change our reality. We will know when an illusion has surfaced because we usually do not FEEL good. Most people respond to this situation with despondency and will tend to wait until the feeling dissipates. In extreme cases this may take a while. Instead, we need to instate a mind set that welcomes each new opportunity to release another layer of illusion. This can be done moments after the realisation that we are not feeling great. The whole process need not take more than a few minutes from start to finish. Each veil cleared takes us a step nearer to manifesting our authentic selves. Times in between the showing of an illusion can be serene and full of fun and joy. If we are particularly in tune we may even be able to sense when the next illusion is about to emerge and clear and deal with it before it gets too big. The slower we are to acknowledge our illusions, the bigger they might need to be to get our attention. It is perfectly possible to clear our stuff without having to go through the mill in the process.

Our illusions or damage effectively obscure our real selves from us and others. Consequently, most of us believe that we ARE our damage. There is often a huge amount of shame and humiliation around this. We do not want others to know about it and judge and criticise us for it. As a result, we have to construct a facade or mask to hide our damage behind, so that other people can be fooled into thinking that we are all right. We tend to choose and cultivate a facade that is as far removed as possible from what we perceive our damage to be. This puts people off the scent and gives us an illusion of being safe and able to function in the world. We are able to keep our facades up most of the time but there are situations where they crack and allow the damage to emerge. These will be moments of stress or provocation. People are often shocked when a monster appears from behind the well cultivated front.

Relationships are one area of life where it is virtually impossible to maintain our facades all the time. Frequently we fall in love with a person's facade. We believe this to be who they are and build our hopes and dreams on this estimation. Many relationships fail due to this alone. When another very different person emerges from behind the facade, we feel cheated and conned. A very common scenario in relationships is when we create a very strong independent facade. This may be either male or female. These people will usually have good jobs, their own home and circle of friends. Others will be attracted to them for these very qualities. This facade is often masking a very needy and dependent person. When these qualities emerge, the suitor will usually run a mile because these are the very elements he or she was trying to avoid.

One facade that women need to be aware of in relationships is the charmer. This man will usually lay on the charm in the courtship phase of the relationship. It will seem as if Prince Charming has arrived to rescue us. However, at the point where a marriage or commitment takes place, a very abusive man may emerge. In my practice I have worked with many women in abusive relationships; in virtually every case they said the partner was charm itself in the early days and they were seduced by this. It is often the hope that the charming man will return that keeps them stuck in the partnership and if they do threaten to leave, he will often turn the charm back on to get her back on side. Ladies be warned!

The fact is that our facades only take us further away from our authentic selves. It is another layer put over it that will need to be dealt with and released. There would be a great deal of fear around letting our facades go. To an extent they become our security blanket. Some of us may even believe that we are our facades and will cling to this for dear life. We can only begin to dismantle our facades when we have cleared enough of the illusions and damage that they were there to mask. This is a gradual process and will happen quite naturally in time. The fact is that our authentic selves are a million times better than any fake persona that we can cultivate. It just takes commitment to release all the aspects of us that we do not like.

We are all consummate actors. The fact is that most of the time we are acting out an illusion so well that we believe it to be real. Not only are we actors worthy of an Oscar but we are also the authors, directors and casting agents in our own particular production. Much of this is done completely unconsciously. Some of us are addicted to high drama and will continually write scripts that live up to this need.

Not only are we casting other people in our personal dramas but they are also casting us in theirs. I have often noticed that with some people I behave in a way that is totally out of character and yet there is an irresistible compulsion to be this way around them. When I first noticed this, it also came to my attention that other people in this person's life were and had also behaved in the same way. I realised that the imprint of her drama and pattern were so strong that anyone who came into the vicinity was sucked into playing out the same role in the drama. This is of course acted out on both sides completely unconsciously. When we become conscious, we can ask ourselves whether we want to play this part and if not, we need to detach from the situation and pull back.

We also put ourselves in a whole variety of roles and we play these based on how we have seen others play them or how we have played them in the past. These roles will be things like mother/father, son/daughter, spouse or lover, worker, friend, sports person and homemaker. If we look at all our various roles, we will act slightly differently. Many people tell me how efficient they are at work, they may manage vast budgets with scrupulous attention to detail and yet when it comes to their own lives they are useless and can't even balance their chequebooks. The role is not the same. We often have one voice that we use at home and very different ones at work or with friends. Some roles we will enjoy more than others and these will probably be the ones that are closer to our authentic selves and need less effort in maintaining. Playing so many parts and trying to keep up with all the various dramas that we are playing out is exhausting. Most of us have no idea who we really are.

Our main objective in becoming our authentic selves is to be in a state of pure being. We don't have to assume a role or impress anyone, we just are. We also do not feel the need to become what other people need or want us to be. We are totally self-accepting.

Most of what we believe ourselves to be is simply ego propaganda. We are being fed a constant diet of our shortcomings and deficiencies. If we believe these, they form a part of the jigsaw puzzle that we create. Many of the things we are told will completely contradict each other and despite making no sense, we still take them on board. To combat this, in response to the ego's judgements and criticism and estimation of us, we have only to ask ourselves if we would like this to be true. If the answer is no, then we have only to discard them and not put them in our composite picture.

Much of our estimation of who we are is created by other people projecting their image onto us. Yet another illusion. This starts at a very early age and is often all we have to go on about who we are. We build up a picture by putting all these inaccurate clues together. The more damaged our parents are, the most distorted and warped our personal image will be. We may need to completely throw out this picture and start from scratch based on our reality and not someone else's.

There is a huge pressure on us to conform by society. We become what everyone else is because we feel like we fit in and our individuality is not challenged. We want to be normal and like others, particularly in our formative and teenage years. People who are different are often bullied or made to feel unacceptable. The fact is that our uniqueness is a huge gift. There is no one else who looks the same and has the gifts and talents that we have. This needs to be celebrated instead of suppressing the parts that make us stand out in a crowd. Most of us only use a fraction of our gifts and abilities because we are so busy living lives that mirror those of everyone around us.

One of our great motivational forces is the need to be

praised and approved of. We often learn at a very young age that if we are and do what Mummy or Daddy wants, we may earn their praise or approval in return. We then have a vested interest in being what they want rather than who we are. This pattern will continue into adulthood. Only the players change. We may want to win the approval of our boss or partner and adapt ourselves to their expectations. We end up losing sight of who we are and end up playing even more roles. It is more important for us to win our own praise and approval for being who we are rather than tying ourselves in knots in an effort to get it from others. **THE ONLY OPINION THAT MATTERS TO ME IS MY OWN.**

IDENTIFYING ROLES

1) Make a list of the roles you have in your life. These will be things like spouse, employee, worker, mother/father, daughter/son, housekeeper, friend, pet owner, artist, agony aunt. etc.

2) Put this list in order of the time you spend being each role.

3) Do you spend more time being what you don't want to be than what you do?

4) Notice if you act slightly differently when playing these various parts. For instance, are you very polite and restrained at work but find you are short tempered at home.

5) Do you like the person that you are when you play these roles?

6) Is there anyone with whom you feel safe enough to completely be yourself? Does this person accept you just as you are?

7) Do you feel that who you are is acceptable to people in all areas of your life?

8) If you had to be honest and describe how you see yourself, how would it be? Write a description.

9) If this contains aspects that you do not like, know that these are part of the illusion and damage from the past and your true authentic self is merely being obscured by it.

10) Begin to get in touch with how your authentic self is and feels. Look at times in your life when you have connected with it. This may be moments like when you see something beautiful like a sunset or lovely view or it may be triggered by the birth of a child or a new relationship. This is a state of being which is filled with a sense of love and joy almost overflowing from you. **THIS IS WHO YOU TRULY ARE AND YOUR NATURAL STATE TO BE IN.**

11) Start dissociating from identifying yourself by your damage or baggage. This is just what you are carrying around with you, not who you are. It would be like seeing a person as the clothes they wear and not by the substance underneath. Just as you can change your clothes, you can choose not to carry the baggage.

12) It may help to stop identifying other people by their baggage. Know that they are also perfect, wonderful, loving children of the light. If you take the attention and energy away from the illusion and put it onto their authentic selves, this will be the part that expands.

13) Have a sense of your authentic self and begin to bring these attributes to all the roles you play. Even if you do not feel it, **FAKE IT UNTIL YOU MAKE IT.**

14) In order to be your authentic self you have to learn to put the ego aside. Be aware of when it is in command

and consciously disconnect from it. Take a deep breath and connect with your true self instead.

TYPES OF FACADES

There are some common facades that we may encounter every day. We may display more than one facade and sometimes different ones come to the forefront in various situations. Remember, we are neither our facades or our damage.

CONTROL FREAK - Will feel powerless and out of control.

FIXER RESCUER - May have had a difficult or traumatic childhood. Tries to rescue others because they want to be rescued.

THE CHARMER - Covers a very damaged, abused and abusive person.

NICE AND HELPFUL - Hides a huge amount of anger. Often takes on a martyr role.

THE ENTERTAINER - Covers feelings of inadequacy and sometimes depression.

THE HEDGEHOG - Prickly on the outside but very soft and vulnerable underneath.

CARING AND SHARING - Very giving externally but tough, demanding and conditional within.

INDEPENDENT - Covers a very needy, dependent personality.

CONFIDENT - Covers feelings of hurt and being let down by people. Makes sure they don't need people.

THE ECCENTRIC - Very sensitive. The eccentricity blocks people from getting too close and hurting them.

THE CASANOVA - Feels insecure and inadequate. Has to score with women in order to hide this.

LITTLE GIRL LOST - Often masks a very tough, manipulative, controlling person.

EFFICIENCY EXPERT - This often hides a chaotic inner dynamic and conflicting emotions and beliefs.

THE SEDUCTRESS - May be afraid of intimacy, has been made to feel hurt and powerless in the past.

THE DO GOODER - Masks feelings of not being good enough and undeserving.

THE CLEVER DICK - Has feelings of inferiority and inadequacy. Needy of praise and approval.

THE WORKAHOLIC - Is afraid of dealing with feelings, can't risk letting anything bring up emotions.

PROCESS FOR ERASING ILLUSIONS

1) You will know when an illusion has been brought to the surface because you do not **FEEL** good.

2) Notice what the feeling is that has emerged. Is it fear, anger, hurt, guilt, jealousy or shame?

3) What has happened to trigger this? Has someone said or done something that has pushed a button? Is this part of a pattern you have or is it an ongoing issue?

4) Recognise that this is an opportunity to let go of a veil of illusion.

5) Breathe out any emotion that is there.

6) Look at what belief systems have been revealed. Command the unconscious mind to delete and erase this belief. Programme a new belief that is in harmony with your authentic self.

7) If this is part of a pattern that constantly repeats, choose to break the cycle.

8) Put in a visual like pulling off the dark veil and

Principle No. 9
YOU ALREADY HAVE AND ARE ALL YOU NEED

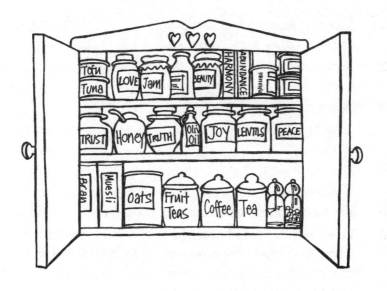

YOU ALREADY HAVE AND ARE ALL YOU NEED

AT THE POINT WHERE WE PERCEIVE THAT WE ALREADY HAVE ALL THAT WE NEED, EVERYTHING BECOMES AVAILABLE TO US.

One of our biggest motivations in life is to get our needs met. It influences our working life, our relationships, our attitude to our family, and our choice of hobbies and interests. A need is something we perceive that we lack and that we are looking to someone or something to provide us with. Some of us have a long list of needs while others may have taught themselves to be more self-sufficient.

The fact is that what we put out, we get back. The universe is very literal. Consequently, if we perceive we have a need for something, we are sending out a message of lack and what we get back is lack. Even if we get the thing we perceive we need, it is never enough because it does not satisfy the inner craving. Need is like a bottomless pit that we never manage to fill up.

Most of what we live and create in our world is an illusion. It is born out of the beliefs and propaganda of the ego. We are so powerful that whatever we believe, we create. This wonderful gift has sadly backfired on us because most of what we manifest comes out of the illusion of lack. The reality is that we are abundant beyond our wildest dreams, there is unlimited bounty available to each and everyone of us. Once we can dispel the illusion of lack, we are free to enjoy the fruits of paradise.

Our needs arise out of what we perceive we did not receive in childhood. We might not have got as much love or been shown it as we wanted. We might not have received praise or approval or been told that we were pretty or clever. We might have felt lonely and isolated and not been given the time or attention we wanted from both our parents. When we grow up we are constantly looking for people to give us these things and to make us feel better about ourselves. Even if the adult aspect of us gets these things, the child within us still perceives a lack which is why nothing is ever enough.

Our needs may also be born out of another illusion, possibly the biggest and most destructive illusion there is, that of SEPARATION. At the point where we perceive ourselves to be separate from our true Divine selves we are plunged into a state of need and lack. We look to external things and people to make up for this. Our higher selves are able to fulfil us and provide most of our needs, it is able to show us how to get the rest of our needs met. When this apparent disconnection takes place, we feel empty and bereft inside. Most addictions come into this category. We try to fill the space with alcohol, cigarettes, drugs, shopping, sex, food, work or many other things. In all these cases there maybe a moment where we feel better and then it is gone. We need more and more of these things to try and recapture this moment but we effectively destroy ourselves in the process.

THERE IS NO PERSON OR THING THAT CAN FILL THE EMPTINESS INSIDE CAUSED BY SEPARATION.

The fact is that the only way to fill the space inside is to reconnect with our true inner selves and feel the love, wisdom, joy and abundance that this part of us brings. We can only have all our needs met if we are connected to the Source of all. If we are not in touch with this part, we are allowing our egos to guide and rule our lives. The ego will feed us fear, lack and the constant demand of our needs. We will be constantly trying and failing to fulfil ourselves with external and material things. In any given moment we will either be sponsored by our true selves or our egos. We will know which mode we are in by how we feel and what we create. However, we have the power of choice to decide which one we want to connect with.

Society is very representative of the ego. It feeds us a sense of inequality and lack. There are haves and have-nots. Society is very judgmental and intolerant of people at all points of the spectrum. Sadly, lack has become so deeply ingrained into our psyches that it is hard to remove this illusion and replace it with the reality of abundance. Lack is nothing to do with how much we have, it is a state of mind. It says that no matter how much we have, it is not enough or that we have to struggle in order to keep it. Society measures a person's worth by what they have and earn and not by who they are.

Needs affect us most in two areas of life, that of abundance and relationships. We will look at both of these separately even though the solution is the same for both areas. My definition of abundance is having more than enough for our needs, wants and desires. Once again it is a state of being rather than a state of bank balance. The fact is that when we are truly abundant we hardly give it a thought, it becomes as natural as breathing. We just know it will be there when we want it. This concept is a long way from the reality that most people in the world experience. We are far more used to struggling to survive and have enough to feed, clothe and shelter ourselves and our families. In our present society most treats and luxuries are often obtained by credit, which reinforces our sense of lack. Many people do jobs that they don't enjoy but are afraid of losing. To me this seems totally irrational to spend half a lifetime doing something that brings no fulfilment or growth but simply a survival wage.

It is ironic that we can only become truly abundant when we know that we already are abundant. As soon as we banish any belief or sense of lack from our lives, we receive everything that we need and want in the perfect moment. There is no fear or worry about how we will manage or if there will be enough in the future. If we look at what we have in our lives, we have a roof over our heads, food and clothes, most of us have televisions, computers, videos, stereo systems, etc. These are not considered to be luxuries but necessities in today's world. When we are in lack whatever we have is not enough, not new enough, big enough, sophisticated enough. We fixate on wanting the things we can't afford instead of being appreciative of what we have.

Abundance encompasses far more than just the material. It is love, friendship, opportunity, creativity, nature and all its bounty, joy and many more qualities. When we know that the material is taken care of, these things assume far greater importance in our lives. Things are expendable, people and nature are not.

When we know that everything is available to us, we actually need and want far less. We don't want to clutter up our lives with things that we don't use or lose interest in as soon as we get them back from the shop. When we no longer have the emptiness inside that we are looking to fill with material things, our needs become simple. I know for myself that when I perceive that I don't have enough money, there are a million and one things that I want and can't afford. I feel deprived and can only see the lack. In contrast, when I perceive that I have more than enough, I can't think of anything important enough to spend my money on. All the things I felt deprived of before seem to disappear. The only thing that has changed is my perception.

Simplicity is a wonderful quality. It means that we remove all extraneous, unnecessary things from our lives and pare it down to the things that matter. We do not waste time or energy on maintaining or doing things that do not enhance our lives. Each individual will have a completely different concept of what simplicity is to them. For some it will seem almost puritanical while others will want a great deal more. We have what we have because it is what we want and not because it is all that we can afford. I use the following guide before buying something. I ask myself, will this thing make my life easier, more comfortable or is it aesthetically pleasing. If it does not fit any of these criteria, I do not buy it.

If we want to make room for new things to come in, we may need to let go of some of the old stuff that we have outgrown or no longer appreciate. There will always be people who will be able to use and enjoy our cast-offs and we may even make some money to pay for the new things.

When we are in a state of abundance, we get all our needs met in the perfect moment. In these circumstances a need is not a projection of what we want but don't have. It is more common that we receive the thing we need before we consciously know that we need it. When it turns up, we are able to see how it fits amazingly into the grand scheme of things. It may be a person, a book, information or the next step on our path. Here we are totally going with the flow and do not anticipate what lies round the next bend, only when we get there do we find the bounty waiting for us.

An essential part of this process is to put the focus of our attention on this moment and not to project our fears and needs into an unknown future. Every time we perceive that all our needs are met in this moment, we pave the way for all our future needs to be fulfilled.

If we are acknowledging that all our needs are being met but think that what we have received is not very good, then we can perhaps look closely at what is needed and why. We might be shown things that do not serve us and need to be healed or changed. We might be shown how we are creating scarcity or lack in our lives and we are being given an opportunity to do it differently. We might have to look for and find the gift of what is being presented to us but it will be there. Once we have acknowledged what the need is and made the changes, the need will no longer be there.

Relationships are the other area where needs play a large part. Most relationships are based on needs and dependency rather than the more romantic ideal of love. We all have a cocktail of needs created out of lack in childhood. We go into relationships with an expectation that our partner will fill all of these needs and we will live happily ever after. In the early phases of a relationship we do our best to give our partner what they need or we may more accurately give them what we need in the hope that they give it back. This is a labour of love and we cannot keep this up as the needs are a bottomless pit. As we get further into the relationship, other priorities take over, children, jobs and the home may become more important than the chore of trying to fulfil other people's needs. This stage will often sound the death knell for the relationship. While we perceive that our partners are meeting fewer of our needs, we pull back on doing and giving them what they need. This tit for tat game will usually result in neither side getting what they think they are in the relationship for so there is very little point in continuing in the partnership.

We can see from this that the whole concept of needs is creating a huge amount of disillusion and pain. Once again

110

the problem is created out of the illusion of need and lack. If we could remove this illusion and replace the whole way in which we perceive relationships with something more obtainable and realistic, life would become much easier to deal with.

We actually cannot expect anyone to meet our needs as they are not real. They are in the child aspect of ourselves, which is why no matter how much we give the adult, it does not feed the child. To eliminate our needs, it is imperative to go to the point where the child first perceived the lack and to change that perception. In order to do this, we must first heal the separation illusion. All the needs that we project onto our partner will tend to give us these things, not because they are needed, expected or demanded but because they are the natural expression of love and affection that the relationship can now be based on.

We tend to base our estimation of ourselves on what people tell us that we are in early life. Any label that is put on us will tend to stick. The fact is that all these beliefs are simply a projection of the other person's stuff. Many parents are of the belief that they should not tell children anything good about themselves as they will become vain and too big for their boots. They also see criticism as a means of improving their children. As a result of all of this we will probably have a very warped view of ourselves. We can only see who we are through other people's eyes. Most of our beliefs about ourselves will be set by the age of five. After that it may be very difficult to shake off these labels no matter how many people try to persuade us otherwise.

Our confidence and self-esteem are created by what other people believe us to be. IN REALITY WE ALREADY ARE THE PERSON WE WOULD MOST LIKE TO BE. Once again we have to remove the veils of illusion that block us from knowing this. If we were to put a composite together of all the qualities and traits we would most like to have, this person will already be living inside us. We simply have to pull off the labels that have been projected and put onto us. It may also help to see where the people who put those labels on were coming from. What were they saying about themselves rather than us? When we can see this, it is much easier to release ourselves from their judgements. Remember **WHAT OTHER PEOPLE THINK OF US IS NONE OF OUR BUSINESS.** We may have to introduce the child within to its true self and create a sense of confidence and high self-esteem based on reality and not projections from other people.

We are constantly being shown people and situations that are simply there to hold up a mirror in front of us to show us what we believe and are manifesting. The mirror image is not necessarily showing us our truth, it is showing us the illusions we have created. If we release the illusion and create the things that we want, then the reflections will also change to mirror our new beliefs.

SIGNS

1) Does your life reflect a state of scarcity and lack?

2) Do you feel that there is never quite enough?

3) Do you do a job that you do not enjoy or does not fulfil you because you need the money to survive?

4) Do you look to someone else to provide you with the things you need?

5) Do you think it is normal to struggle?

6) What needs do you expect your partner to fulfil?

7) Do you suppress your needs in order not to be vulnerable or hurt?

8) Do you see traits and qualities in others that you would like to have?

TIPS FOR HAVING WHAT WE NEED AND WANT

1) Make a list of your needs, wants and desires.
2) How many of these do you manage to get consistently in your life?
3) Do you need others to provide these or can you get them for yourself?
4) Look at the family patterns around lack. Were you programmed as a child to see that there was not enough? Do you choose to continue these patterns?
5) Look at and make a list of your personal patterns around lack.
6) Begin to bring in abundance perception. Focus on all the good things you are provided with. Make sure these loom larger than any sense of lack.
7) TRUST that everything you need is provided in the perfect moment.
8) Do not project any fear, worry or lack into the future. Stay in the moment and see all the good that you have right now.
9) Do you project your needs onto your partner and then feel resentful when he/she does not manage to fulfil them in the way you would like? Is this creating tension within your relationships? Look at your list of needs and see which ones you are most insistent that they meet.
10) What were the circumstances of childhood that have

created these needs?

11) Look at ways in which to remove the needs from your partner by finding ways to be responsible for

   fulfilling these needs or changing any perception that you do not already have these things.

12) How do you see yourself?

13) What labels were put onto you that you are believing? e.g. stupid, ugly, lazy, selfish, bad or wicked.

14) Who were the people who told you these things?

15) Note that these labels were a projection of how these people felt about themselves. They may even have had these labels slapped onto them.

16) Make a list of the traits and qualities that you would like to have. How many of these do you demonstrate even in a small way?

17) What stands in the way of you living all these things on a daily basis? e.g. confidence, fear.

18) Choose to know that these blocks are an illusion and do not exist in reality. Let them go.

19) KNOW that you already are and have everything that you need want and desire.

THE PROCESS FOR HEALING SEPARATION AND CHILDHOOD ISSUES

1) In advance of doing this process have your list of needs and labels to hand.

2) Be willing to accept that the source of all needs is

within and not without.

3) Take some time and space where you will not be disturbed or distracted.

Sit comfortably in a chair and begin to take some deep breaths to relax your body and still your mind. You are going to go back in time to the child inside and heal any illusions that have been created and are blocking your life and growth. Find out from the unconscious mind how old you were when you separated from the Divine within. For many of us this seems to be before birth while we are in the womb. This is often due to the emotions and circumstances that surround pregnancy. If a mother is in fear, worry or anger this may extend to the baby and may appear to disconnect it from the Divine source. You are now going to go back in time within the unconscious mind to the point in your development where the separation took place. See that from this point on you are in a state of lack, struggle and survival. The person who is going to create the healing is you the adult. Explain to the little baby that it has not been abandoned but it has simply unplugged itself form the Divine source and you are going to help it reconnect. There are three points of connection. Firstly the solar plexus, this is the centre of power and wisdom. There is a vast globe of energy and light. See that plug go into the centre of this and feel that golden energy flow into your solar plexus, filling up this space. See the energy spilling over and radiating all around the little baby, creating a wonderful aura. The next connection point is the heart and the source of all love. See the chord and disconnected plug once again. The energy of love has a pale pink tone to it. See the source of eternal love as this massive pinky white orb and put the plug into the centre of it. Feel this beautiful loving energy coursing into you through the heart and travelling to every single cell of the body. Sense this love, warmth and comfort and see it

115

overflowing from you to touch those around. The final connection to make is from the crown of the head. This is the pure brilliant white light that communicates, feeds and nurtures us. Send out that chord and plug into the source of this energy. Feel the amazing pure energy entering your body from the top of your head and filling the whole of the body. Any of these energies used or given away will be immediately replaced. The illusion of emptiness will have disappeared. We are filled full with these amazing energies. Explain to the little one inside that these will provide ALL its needs and it does not have to demand what it needs from people who may be unable to give them. When the baby has its own needs met, life becomes about what it can give rather than about what it wants. See this baby thriving and glowing, no matter what the external circumstances of life are. These things do not touch it as it does not take them personally. You are now going to move forward in time to the three or four year old. Look at what beliefs this child has about itself based on the words or actions of those around it. See the metaphorical labels that have been stuck on the child. Explain to the child that many of these are not real and apply more to the people who stuck them on than they do to it. Together you can pull off any label that you do not like or does not fit in with who you want to be. Throw these labels onto a bonfire and see them burn. Take this child onto your lap and give it a big hug. Let it know how much you love it and how proud of it you are. Let it know all the wonderful qualities it has so that it has a clear image of itself through your eyes. See its confidence and self-esteem grow, not in a big headed way but because it knows that there is nothing wrong, bad or not good enough about it. This confidence just glows out from the child, it does not need to broadcast it. See the child playing happily, in total harmony with itself, with its surroundings and nature and totally connected with the inner source. Finish by reassuring it that if it disconnects or forgets who it is, you will be there to

Principle No. 10
ACCEPTANCE

ACCEPTANCE

Acceptance is a principle that, if mastered, will reap huge rewards. Acceptance says that whoever we are and whatever is going on around us is just fine in this moment. It sees what is good and makes the best of what is on offer. Acceptance is yet another principle that will have to be learned and practised as our society does not show us how to be accepting and is more likely to focus on what is not working for us.

Acceptance is the key to happiness. Without acceptance, happiness is always going to remain just out of our reach. When we bring in acceptance, we put happiness under our own control. We are not reliant on others to create the conditions for our joy and where there is a possibility of being let down. We can make the decision to be happy and not simply wait powerlessly for it to come to us. It also takes the pressure off others to provide our happiness, which is a very tall order.

With acceptance we learn not to engage with the things that are not as we would like them to be in an ideal world. Nothing is going to be perfect and yet things will be just right for where we are and where the world is at this stage of its evolution. We have to bring in detachment so that we can observe people and situations without becoming emotionally involved in them.

Everything in life is created from energy. Energy wants to flow. When we do not have acceptance, we will create a block to that flow. We want things to be different from how they are and therefore we try to manipulate the energy to be how we want it, rather than how it is. This of course never works and only creates struggle. Without acceptance it is impossible to go with the flow and reap the benefits that are on offer to us.

Control and acceptance are completely incompatible bedfellows. When we have the need to exert control over others, we are coming from a position of fear and insecurity. This will only be reinforced by our inability to make others be the way we want them to be. It is much easier to want what we have got rather than to get what we want. The former brings in acceptance and the latter control. Wants are coming from a position of lack and this will usually be what we get back.

There are three main areas in which we need to employ acceptance. First, we can accept ourselves just as we are. Secondly, we can accept other people without judgements or criticism and finally, we can learn to accept the things that are presented to us in our outer world. We will look at these three aspects separately.

Learning to accept ourselves is probably one of the hardest things we can do. We will have a long list of things that we believe to be unacceptable about ourselves. Some of these will be on a physical level, some will be defects in our personality and others will be areas where we perceive ourselves to be not good enough. The ego will feed us all our flaws and shortcomings on a daily basis. Society does not help in this area. It gives such a narrow view of how we should be that only a minority of people will ever fit it. This is particularly predominant in our appearance. For the most part our physicality and looks are determined by our genes. We are not consciously involved in the selection process. It is therefore ridiculous to create a climate where only certain looks are acceptable. This has caused untold damage particularly in the western world. It has reached a point where even the few people who do fit the criteria think that parts of their bodies are unacceptable or are having to wage a constant battle against the ageing process. In bringing in acceptance, we can learn to buck this very destructive trend. It is a great deal cheaper than plastic surgery!

The fact is that other people will mirror back to us our thoughts and feelings about ourselves. When we accept ourselves just as we are, others will as well. Not buying into the "body perfect" trend will help to eliminate struggle in our lives and set us free from one of the most tyrannical elements in our society.

Learning to accept our physical looks is only stage one in self-acceptance. Next we need to deal with who we are. Remember, who we believe ourselves to be will be distorted by our damage and the damage of those who were involved in our development. Who we are is exactly who we are meant to be for the challenges, growth and learning we have come to work with. We have a unique set of gifts and abilities that will enable us to overcome any difficulties we may face. Also, we are in a constant state of evolution. If we were to look back at ourselves ten or twenty years ago, we can see how far we have come. There is a great deal for us still to learn but we can bring in acceptance of the point we are right now. We are after all work in progress and new elements will come into play along the way.

We are often so hard on ourselves and part of the road to self-acceptance will involve taming the ego and not believing any of its negative propaganda. This is much easier said than done. We can counter any judgements with a statement like I LOVE AND ACCEPT MYSELF JUST AS I AM. We may not believe this in the early days but gradually we can integrate this understanding into our very being. We may also need to do some work on releasing patterns and beliefs that do not resonate with this. We choose the reality we want to create!

Learning to accept others will work hand in hand with

self-acceptance. The more we are able to accept ourselves, the less we will need to project our inadequacy onto others. Accepting other people does not mean that they all have to become our bosom buddies. There may be a basic incompatibility. We do not make them wrong for who they are. We live and let live.

Relationships are a key area where acceptance needs to be brought in. It is true to say that it is probably the most important element in a successful partnership. We go into relationships with a whole bunch of expectations, needs and demands. Most relationships break up because we are unable to meet these. We set the standard for the union at such a high level that it may be impossible to reach it in any consistent way. When we bring in acceptance, we are coming from a much more realistic perspective. We are aware of the flaws and shortcomings of our partner and we accept them rather than trying to change them. We allow where we are at in the relationship to be just fine. We do not put any pressure on our partners to be anything other than who they are. We choose to love and accept them just as they are. It is important to note that there is some behaviour in a relationship that is unacceptable. This may include things like abuse, violence or serial adultery. When these things occur, it may be time to dissolve the partnership rather than learning to accept these actions.

Many of us fall in love with a person's potential rather than who they are at the time. Sadly, very few of us ever manage to live up to our potential. In the early days of a relationship we always show ourselves in our most positive light. As we become more comfortable together, we bring in other aspects of our personality that are perhaps rather unsavoury. This is where acceptance will need to be employed. We also need to acknowledge that who a person presents themselves to be at the beginning of the union is not the full picture and not to be surprised or disappointed when the other person begins to emerge. In my opinion this is where a relationship really starts and while the early phase is very enjoyable, it is not necessarily the reality and should be recognised as such.

It is often the little things in a relationship that end up becoming the final straw. This could be things like the way they eat, leaving clothes or towels on the floor, leaving the toilet seat up or other hygiene or bathroom habits. While these may seem petty, they often become the focus of other issues within the partnership. This is a very challenging area for bringing in acceptance. We can decide to perceive our partner's habits as endearing or amusing. We may need to detach from the things first and stop plugging into them and finding them irritating. We may also need to remind ourselves that we will also do things that will be equally annoying to our partner. The more love we feel for our partner, the easier it will be to bring in acceptance for the things they do or do not do.

Humour will be one of our best tools in learning to accept other people. When we choose to be amused rather than offended or critical, not only do we get more out of the situation but we take the negative charge out of it.

The main way in which we show our lack of acceptance of others is through judgements and criticism. These may be voiced or unvoiced. We may use judgements as a means of protecting ourselves. To make others less is a way of seeing ourselves as being more acceptable in comparison. This is of course an illusion. At the end of the day we are all one and what we do to others, we do to ourselves. Judging and criticising is a very addictive habit and we might get quite a lot of pleasure from it. We may enjoy doing it with friends in the form of gossip. We may not be able to break the addiction by going cold turkey. It will be a question of bringing in some awareness and catching ourselves in the judgement or criticism and turning it around by mentally stating I ACCEPT ... JUST AS HE/SHE IS. We can gradually wean ourselves off the urge to judge. It is essential that we are not too hard on ourselves when we do not manage it. It has become so deeply ingrained in our human nature that we will not shift it overnight.

Accepting external situations is another very challenging aspect of this principle. Essentially we come from a position of powerlessness when dealing with our outer world. We cannot control the things that are beyond our personal space. If we do not have acceptance of things in our outer world, we will constantly be angry, frustrated, disappointed and dissatisfied.

In bringing in acceptance for the outside world, it is essential to firstly remove any expectations of how we think things "should" be. We can then open our minds to ALL possibilities. Very often what we get is far better for us than what we expected or thought we wanted.

Some of the external circumstances we are faced with will be quite demanding. This may include things like the death or illness of a loved one, redundancy or divorce. If we do not bring in acceptance of these things, we risk staying stuck in struggle. We cannot move on or reap the benefits that may be on offer to us. If we rail against what we are being presented, we will stay in the anger and hurt and this is a dreadful place to be. Often the bigger challenge, the greater the opportunity we are being given. This includes the death of a close relative. They may be freeing us up to enjoy a new phase of life. If we cannot accept this, we may miss the boat and the gesture would have been for nothing.

Travel is a wonderful arena for bringing in acceptance

of external events. No matter what mode of transport we choose, there will be a whole load of elements that are completely beyond our control. This makes travelling a rather fraught and stressful pastime. We have probably all been in situations where we have a deadline or appointment and we are stuck in traffic. Our blood pressure goes up and our language may become quite colourful. By the time we reach our destination, we are so uptight. In my experience, whenever this happens all my negative energy has been for nothing. If I am late, I often find that the other person is also running late and I arrive at the perfect time. There may also be a gift for the person I am meeting in my lateness. When we bring in this trust and acceptance, we can relax, put some music on and have some time with our own thoughts. We might need to program in the acceptance. We could have a phrase to hand like I ACCEPT THAT I WILL REACH MY DESTINATION AT THE PERFECT TIME FOR ALL INVOLVED.

We can employ acceptance every day. When we get up we can have a loose framework for our day. There will often be unforeseen events that crop up or things that fall by the wayside. We can flow with any changes and choose to see the gift in these changes.

The weather will often challenge our acceptance resolve. We cannot control or alter it and consequently we have to go with it. We may need to be flexible with our plans if they are dependent on certain weather conditions. We can learn to create a win for ourselves no matter what Mother Nature has up her sleeve. A wet, rainy day can mean snuggling up in front of the fire with a good book or video. A sunny day can involve a picnic or long walk.

There may be some world events that may be quite hard to accept. This may be war, terrorism, earthquakes or other natural disasters. We may not be able to see the big picture and so we get caught up in the pain, loss and suffering. We may need to employ detachment here, without losing any compassion. The fact is that if we over-empathise or relate too strongly to these things, we are unnecessarily adding to the fear and pain in the world instead of trying to eliminate it.

The indications that we are not using acceptance will be stress, anger, fear, hurt, jealousy and powerlessness. These are all aspects of our lives that we would like to eradicate and acceptance is the key to achieving this.

We only need to use acceptance for the things that it is not in our power to change at the moment. There are a great many things we can alter to suit ourselves without interfering with other people's choices. For instance, if there is an aspect of our home or garden that we would like to be different, we have only to paint walls, rearrange furniture or plant some new flowers. We can sometimes be so passive or stuck that we do not make simple changes that would give us a better quality of life. This may also include things like jobs, friends or things that are past their sell by date. It is simple enough to instigate changes in these areas rather than bringing in acceptance. We may need to acknowledge the fears that are stopping us from moving on.

We are always in a state of evolution. This means that there is a constant climate of change. The acceptance that we have is for this moment only. We will need to embrace the changes and learn to accept them as well. We are always in a state of flow. This is why acceptance is something that we do once and that is it. We are constantly having to reassess and create new understandings and belief systems. If we hold onto old outdated patterns, we end up damming the flow and slowing down our speed of evolution.

We can also block our growth by our refusal to accept aspects of ourselves or our lives. **WHAT WE RESIST PERSISTS.** We may only be able to move on and make changes when we acknowledge what IS right now. We cannot change anything that we are in denial over. Denial and acceptance are very different but may be confused. One refuses to admit that something exists while the other allows it to be as it is for the present. A way in which this might show itself would be in a relationship. One partner may be in denial that there are aspects of the relationship that are not working. They may even pretend in their own minds that everything is perfect. Instead, they could accept the relationship as it is but see the aspects that are not satisfactory and need to be worked on. From this standpoint they can either clear any issues or acknowledge that they have outgrown each other and it is time to move on.

Acceptance is always a choice that we make and once again it will need to be practised before it is mastered. We feel so much better for bringing in acceptance that this can galvanise us into bringing it into more areas of our lives. When we are in total acceptance, we are not blocking the flow of energy of life in any way. We are open to all possibilities and we are not weighing down our energy with emotions like anger, fear, hurt and jealousy.

TIPS FOR BRINGING IN ACCEPTANCE

1) Acknowledge that if you want happiness to be a part of your life, acceptance will need to be mastered.

2) Look at the things that you can change and choose to accept the ones that you can't.

3) Do you try to control people and events in order to make them be what you want? How much success do you have with this? Let go and decide to want what you have rather than waste energy by trying to get what you want.

4) Look at how often you have expectations about people and events. You will usually be disappointed as things seldom live up to expectations. Instead, choose to go in with an open mind and **ACCEPT** whatever comes along as the best thing for this moment in time.

5) Do you enjoy a good moan? Notice if you put your attention on all the things that are wrong rather than what is working for you. Bring in acceptance if you catch yourself having a whinge.

6) Is stress part of your life? A lack of acceptance will greatly contribute to stress. Learn to accept the things that you cannot change.

TIPS FOR BRINGING IN SELF-ACCEPTANCE

1) What parts of yourself do you find it hard to accept? (These are not just on the physical.)

2) Do you attempt to hide or change these things?

3) Do other people tease you or remark on them? Are you in denial over these areas?

4) Could you imagine loving these parts of you?

5) Do you put yourself down to other people?

6) Do you allow others to judge and criticise you?

7) Do you envy people who have the things you want?

8) What feelings are brought up by your lack of

acceptance of these areas?

9) Is there a reason why you may be challenged in this area? (**A** chosen life lesson.)

10) What means do you have to overcome any difficult aspects of yourself?

11) Do you use these things to punish or beat yourself up?

12) Do you think you deserve not to love and accept yourself?

13) Do you resist seeing the issue for what it is and therefore accepting it?

14) Accept that you are exactly as you are meant to be for what you are here to learn.

15) What you resist persists. Is there a part of yourself you are stuck in struggle with? Choose to let go and see if things can change.

16) Affirm that you love and accept yourself just as you are.

TIPS FOR ACCEPTING OTHERS

1) Who are the people you find it hardest to accept? Make a list in order of importance in your life. e.g. spouse, children, parents, siblings, boss etc.

2) What are the specific things that get to you most about them? Some of these will seem very petty like leaving socks on the floor.

3) Check out whether any of these things are simply showing a mirror of what needs to be released or healed within you. If so this is your issue and once it is dealt with, the reflection will not be there.

4) Are some of these things habits or idiosyncrasies that this person has? These are things you can learn to accept. Choose to find these things amusing or endearing rather than irritating.

5) If the things that you find unacceptable in others are born out of their damage from the past, choose to bring in compassion and understanding with the acceptance.

6) Make sure you are not projecting your own stuff onto your children. Let them be who they are rather than who you want them to be. Choose to accept and love them just as they are.

7) In learning to accept and forgive your parents, you need to bring in one truth. **I ACCEPT THAT MY PARENTS DID THEIR ABSOLUTE BEST FOR ME WITH THE RESOURCES AND UNDERSTANDING THAT WAS AVAILABLE TO THEM AT THE TIME.**

8) With people in general, know that if you feel anger, hurt, jealousy or frustration, you are not accepting them. When you bring in acceptance, these emotions will not be there.

9) Be aware of your judgements and criticism of others. Know that you may be using these as a form of protection.

10) Set yourself the task of not indulging in judgements or criticism. Allot a period of time where you will monitor your thoughts and cancel any that are derogatory. Gradually increase these periods of time as you become more adept.

11) Have an acceptance statement to hand like **I ACCEPT...... JUST AS HE/SHE IS.**

TIPS FOR ACCEPTING EXTERNAL EVENTS

1) Choose to let go of any expectations about how things should be or any specific outcomes.

2) If you are challenged by things that you would not want to happen, you may need to find the gift before you are able to bring in acceptance.

3) Allow everyday irritations of life to wash over you. This may be traffic jams or things not going to plan.

4) Do you have stress in your life? If so, you are not employing acceptance. Look at what is important and set your priorities. Ask yourself, if you look back in ten years time, will this be significant in the grand scheme of things? Family and health have to take precedence over work deadlines.

5) Accept whatever Mother Nature has up her sleeve. Flow with the weather and the seasons.

Principle No. 11
TRUST

TRUST

Trust is one of the most useful qualities that we can access. It completely frees us to enjoy life to the full because we know that everything is taken care of. Once again, this is not something we are taught as children and consequently it is a skill we have to learn.

Trust is the antidote to fear, worry and doubt. This is the most important role that it can play in our lives. We know how destructive fear and worry can be. They take over our minds and dominate and limit our existence. Fear and worry are always about things that may or may not happen in the future. This will often be based on our past experiences. We believe that if something has happened before, it is likely to recur. We remember how it felt last time and we project these feelings into our future. The fact is that the majority of the things we fear and worry about will never happen. The things that do occur can only be dealt with as and when they appear. This we often do admirably and there will be a great deal of growth and gifts to be gained from the situations, so we would not want to deny ourselves these.

Fear is an illusion and trust will be the thing that dispels that illusion. Fear is also a choice that we make and in bringing in trust we are showing that we have made the decision not to be fearful. Trust is our link to the Divine truth that says there is nothing to fear but fear itself. It knows that anything that happens will be for a good reason that is ultimately for our highest good. This may seem hard to believe when we see so much pain and suffering in the world. We have to remember that much of this is born out of our freedom to choose our reality and this is what many people choose because they do not know any different. This is why it is essential to educate and introduce the concept that there are other ways to live that can eliminate pain, suffering and struggle from our existence.

Trust hands the remote control for our lives to a higher power that will not let us down or lead us astray. Where there is a need for control, there is an absence of trust. Control freaks will have usually experienced being controlled by others and see this as the only other option available to them. At the point where we hand over control to our higher selves, we know that everything is taken care of. We can relax and enjoy the journey knowing that the person at the helm can direct our route and the safest possible way to negotiate it.

Abundance is another area that requires trust. It is probably true to say that our level of abundance is commensurate with the trust that we have in the universe to provide for us. I must stress here that abundance is not determined by the amount of money we have. It is more the understanding that everything we need and want is available to us. This is not just material things. It may be love, joy, creative fulfilment or many other things. This is one area that often foils people. We may think that to be abundant we have to work harder or get a job with better prospects. We often fail to see all the ways in which we can be given what we need. Consequently, we may well block these potential avenues of abundance. Trust will not provide us with the specific means by which our abundance will occur, we need to be open to all eventualities.

Trust is one of the hardest lessons that we have come to master. It needs to become part of our being and not just something that we pay lip service to. It is very easy to say and affirm that we trust but if the underlying feelings do not reinforce this, then the words are pretty empty. The biggest challenge to our trusting will once again be the ego. Even as we try to instil trust, it will often counter it with doubts, giving examples from the past where we have been let down. The ego will also tell us how stupid we are to believe this rubbish in the first place. The more dominant our ego is, the harder it will be to instate trust. It may be necessary to do some work on disempowering the ego so that it does not have such a hold on us. We will know when we have managed to master trust and get it past the ego's defences because we feel it rather than just think it. It is knowing that it comes from our very core and not something purely on an outer level.

Trust does not mean that we automatically trust everyone and everything. Far from it. As we have all learnt many times, people let us down, betray us and fail to live up to our expectations. We are often quick to criticise those who give their trust too easily to people. They are often walked over and hurt along the way. There are two areas where we can safely place our trust. Firstly, on the higher self and also on ourselves in the form of the intuition.

Our higher selves are all knowing, wise, loving and nurturing. They will not let us down and only want the absolute best for us. Therefore, it is completely safe to give our trust to this powerful aspect of ourselves. To do this we have to connect with it and build a close and loving relationship. This is something that grows with time and commitment. As it grows, so does the trust we are able to give to it. We will also notice that the ease in which we are able to live our lives will also grow with this relationship. Our ultimate aim is to become one with this part of us and live at the optimal level that is available. This of course is work in progress.

The higher self will communicate to us through our intuition. This is where we need to give our trust to ourselves and the information we receive. An incident happened to me that demonstrated this. I was driving on a three lane motorway in the fast lane. I noticed that the middle lane was clear and so I went to move over. An inner voice clearly told me to stay where I was and I even felt the car resisting my attempt to change lanes. I immediately looked to see the reason for this message. There was a juggernaut in the slow lane opposite where I was but there was nothing in front of it, so there would be no reason for it to change lanes. Despite logic and my ego trying to convince me that my caution was unnecessary, I did heed the message and the juggernaut did swerve into the middle lane and I would have been right in its blind spot. I learned a huge lesson that day. It also helped me to see how my higher self wants to keep me safe and avoid any unnecessary pitfalls along the way.

We have to learn to distinguish between the ego voice and the intuitive one. As our relationship with the higher self grows, this becomes easier. It is like when a loved one phones, they don't have to identify themselves. The voice is so familiar. We also need to keep the channels of communications open so that any guidance is able to reach us at the appropriate time. The way in which we need to employ trust in using our intuition is firstly by believing the validity of the information and then by acting upon it. Sometimes it may be an incredibly illogical thing to do. The ego will of course try and convince us that we have lost the plot totally. However, trusting and acting upon intuition will always payoff. We may not be shown the payoff until after the action is in place. Part of the trust is to know that there will be one.

We will often use the word "hope" and it may seem as

if this is a positive word. However, the word has a great deal of doubt built in. It says "this is what I would like to happen but frankly I am not terribly confident." Hope will test negatively in muscle testing. We tend to use this word a great deal and it is necessary to substitute it with trust. When we program trust into something, it gives the universe a fait accompli that will send it back to us. When we give it doubt, it will send doubt right back. This will only reinforce a sense of lack and powerlessness.

Trust is like a muscle that needs to be exercised. It is not enough to bring it in once and think that this will do the job. Our trust also needs to be proactive rather than reactive. It is not just about calling it in when we find ourselves in a sticky situation. Rather it is about bringing it in beforehand so that it is already in place and will help to carry us through any challenges that we may encounter along the way. Trust can become part of our daily ritual, just like cleaning our teeth. After a while, it will become part of our being. This does not have to be hard work or a drudge. It takes just a moment to connect with this energy and put it in place. This then frees us up to enjoy our day knowing that anything we need will be supplied to us in the perfect moment.

Trust can also be employed when we find ourselves in a quandary or situation that has no obvious solution. It may be that the answer has not yet been created. When we encounter these situations, we simply hand the problem over to the higher self and trust that the solutions will present itself when the time is right. This may go against the grain and the ego will tell us that it is a cop out. We are so used to wrangling and wrestling with a problem and fretting and worrying about it. I must stress here that it is not the same as burying our heads in the sand and not dealing with it. We are totally aware of the issue but at this point in time it is beyond us, therefore there is nothing to be done until the answer arrives.

Trust is the key to freedom. This is a quality that we all profess to want. We can only be totally free when we are no longer imprisoned by lack, fear, anguish and loss. Trust allows us to push back the limitations that our fear has imposed upon us and to know that everything is possible.

Trust is in complete harmony with the rhythm and flow of life. It knows that nothing that cannot be replaced is ever lost forever and no one can do anything to us that we do not on some level allow. It knows that ultimately there is only love in the world and everything that is not born out of love is an illusion that we do not have to buy into and manifest in our lives. Trust knows that if a job, relationship, baby or move is not forthcoming, then it is not right for us at this time. There is no need for frustration or angst in these areas.

Embracing trust in our lives will as ever involve a degree of awareness. We can notice when our thoughts, words and actions are buying into fear and worry and reinforcing negative beliefs that we then manifest in reality. Once we are conscious of our lack of trust, we can begin to choose to let it go and embrace trust in its place. This may involve having a trust statement to hand like I TRUST THAT MY NEEDS, WANTS AND DESIRES ARE PROVIDED IN THE PERFECT MOMENT. Breathe this understanding into the inner self. There may be a moment when we can feel the trust kick into the body. This is quite a subtle feeling. It is a sense of peace and calm replacing any fear, doubt and worry.

When we instate trust into our lives, we will find that it becomes a magnet that attracts all sorts of miracles and good things to us. These are not necessarily things we have put out for but we will find that they are usually exactly what we need, when we need it. We may not even see the need until the means to meet it has arrived.

TIPS FOR BRINGING IN TRUST

1) Become aware of your thoughts and words. Are they being sponsored by fear of love?

2) Are you a chronic worrier? Does your mind always jump to a worst case scenario and you feel as if this thing is already happening? Do you worry as a means of punishing yourself or distracting you from your life work?

3) It takes discipline to bring in trust and let go of fear and worry. You may need to commit yourself to this.

4) Have a trust statement to hand for when you notice you have got on a worry train. Halt it in its tracks by repeating the statement until the worry subsides. Some good affirmations are:-

I TRUST THAT I HAVE EVERYTHING I NEED OR WANT IN THE PERFECT MOMENT.

I TRUST I AM SAFE AT ALL TIMES.

I TRUST I AM TAKEN CARE OF.

I TRUST MY LIFE IS PERFECT JUST AS IT IS.

5) In the early stages of this process you may find that you have to instate a trust affirmation every time a fear arises. As trust becomes embedded in your being, you will need to do this less and less until eventually it will just be there without any need for reinforcement. This is the goal to aim for.

6) Don't just wait to bring in trust in reaction to something. Inject trust into your day in advance. Build it into your morning ritual of getting up and ready for the day. You may need to put up a post it

note in a place you are bound to see it to remind you.

7) You are giving your trust to your higher self and your intuition. Remember to keep the channels of communication open so that you can be reached at any time.

8) Listen to what your intuition has to say and make sure the ego does not try to override it or make you feel stupid for believing it.

9) Always act upon your intuition or the whole process will be for nothing.

10) When you have a problem that has no obvious solution, hand it over to your higher self and trust that it will be sorted at the right time and in the right way. Then let it go. Wait and see what presents itself.

11) Be aware that not everyone is worthy of your trust. Don't give your power away to others and check in with your intuition as to the reliability of anyone you encounter. Listen to what it tells you even if the person seems to be wonderful on the outside. The intuition will penetrate far deeper than the surface and the facade.

12) Notice if and when you use the word "hope." Catch yourself and immediately replace it with trust.

13) Allow trust to let you go with the flow and to embrace all the experiences of life, knowing that you are safe and taken care of at all times.

14) Use trust to open the door to freedom. Freedom from the tyranny of fear and lack.

Principle No.12
JOY, FUN, LAUGHTER AND BREATH

JOY, FUN, LAUGHTER AND BREATH.

Although this is the final principle, it is by no means the least important. It is the natural consequence of bringing the other principles into practice. We are all looking for joy and happiness and yet these may be very illusive qualities that we often look to other people and external situations to provide.

We cannot help being in a state of joy when we are at one with everything around us, when we are no longer living out destructive illusions, when we see the good in everything with which we are presented and when we know that we are so powerful that we can create whatever we want and that we are looked after at the highest levels and when we know that who we are is fantastic and wonderful.

All the clearing, growing and learning that we experience in life is geared to return us to our natural state of being, which is to be loved and loving, happy, abundant, fulfilled in our life work, creative and wise. All these qualities emerge and integrate more and more as we progress along our path.

Joy, fun and laughter are not simply the reward we get when we reach our destination, they are an essential part of the journey. We are meant to have a good time in the process of life. So many people take their spiritual journey very seriously and think it is being trivialised if we inject fun and humour into it. This could not be further from the truth. This is possibly a legacy from times when a spiritual life involved suffering, hardship and abstention from anything pleasurable. Monks and nuns of old believed that this was how God wanted to be served. The greater the suffering, the more grace that would be created in Heaven. This belief was so deeply ingrained that it may be difficult to shake it off. We may think that there is something noble about suffering and abstinence and that we will be rewarded for it. The truth is that pain will lower our spirits, while fun and laughter will raise them. This is surely our whole purpose on Earth.

In the past we have mainly learned our lessons through pain. This is not because this was what we deserved but simply because it would take something quite big to get our attention and show us the lessons we are being given. If life is going along swimmingly, we do not look to see what we are being taught. We have been so unconscious that it might take quite a big issue to pierce that consciousness. Things are changing now, there is a universal consciousness that is now taking hold and we can learn our lessons through pleasure and not pain. To do this we have to be aware of when and how our lessons are being presented to us. This may be quite subtle. In my experience, significant issues show themselves in groups of three. I might miss the message the first time it is shown, the second time a bell will sound and I begin to take note and the third time is the confirmation that makes me look at what I am being told. This can all be done with joy and not angst. I see it a bit like trying to solve a puzzle or conundrum. There can be a huge amount of satisfaction to be gained from this.

Many of the old sayings contain more than a grain of truth. LAUGHTER IS THE BEST MEDICINE is one of these. It has actually been scientifically proven that when we laugh, the body produces healing chemicals and feel-good hormones. There is a well known case of a man who upon finding that he had a serious cancer, decided to treat it with laughter. He got videos of his favourite comedies and watched them until the cancer went away.

Laughter does not just heal physical problems, it also has the power to lift emotional ailments like depression and bereavement.

Laughter will lift almost any situation and lighten the energy and atmosphere. It is the way to get through difficult or challenging periods of our lives. We can **CHOOSE** to see the funny side of almost everything. It will put a positive charge onto the issue and take away a great deal of negativity. We can also choose to be amused by the traits and habits in people that would normally irritate and annoy us.

My motto of life is **IF IT ISN'T FUN, DON'T DO IT.** This does not mean that nothing gets done that is mundane or boring. Rather, I would look for ways to make these tasks more enjoyable. I might put some music on or get friends round and turn it into a party.

Balance is one of the most important things we can achieve. We need to find a balance between our adult and child selves. However, we do need to make sure that our child is healed and happy and does not carry the wounds from childhood. If this has not been done, the child aspect may be needy and unhappy rather than full of fun and joy. Our adult selves work with the mind and logic and are very good at getting things done and organised. The child works with emotions and will have a great capacity for learning, discovery and adventure. We can see that when these two aspects of us work in harmony together, we are a formidable force to be reckoned with.

If we look at some of the most highly evolved creatures in the world like dolphins, whales and dogs, we can see that play is a very important element in their daily existence. This is not limited to the infant stage either. Adult animals spend a great deal of their time playing. This should give us a clue as to how to live our lives. We need to incorporate play into our everyday schedules. Some people save it all up for a two week holiday once a year and the rest of the time is spent grafting in order to pay for it. Many people find that they are too tired to do anything that they enjoy after a hard day's work. This is when we are out of balance. If we do things that we enjoy, we become energised. It is only the things we don't enjoy that drain us.

We have to an extent been brainwashed by society to believe that we are not meant to enjoy or love what we do to earn a living. It is a means to an end. Consequently many people do not look to their choice of career to provide them with joy, fun and laughter, rather they may be more concerned with the pay structure. There is also a belief that we cannot earn enough to live on from the things we enjoy like our hobbies. I am firmly of the belief that we are meant to do what we love and enjoy and get rewarded for it as well. This may take a while to filter through to general consciousness but if enough people live this, the domino effect can take place.

Life is too important to be taken seriously. The author Maya Angelou hit the nail on the head when she said that she did not want just to survive but to thrive with passion, compassion, humour and style. The perfect combination!

Humour can be used as a cover up or protection. Many comedians use laughter to mask very dark or depressive feelings. It is their facade. This is not what I am advocating. Fun and laughter need to be a part of our very core being. They can bubble out from us and touch and positively affect anyone who comes into our vicinity.

Many people are not comfortable with feeling and expressing emotions. This is often due either to the fact that negative emotions were not tolerated within childhood or there was a great deal of negativity within the family. We then look for ways in which to disconnect from our feelings as it may be too painful to be in touch with them. One of the most common ways of doing this is to escape into the logical mind. We try to keep busy and work with figures, logic or machines where we can be in control. Computer games and the Internet feed this pattern. This may be more predominant with men than women and it is very destructive to relationships and family life. The fact is that when we suppress our negative emotions, we also have to push down our positive ones like love and joy. When we are only functioning on a mind level, we can become rather like a robot.

When emotions are suppressed, they are going to give us problems in some areas of life. They may attack the body and cause illness or ailments. They may explode out in dangerous ways like road rage or aggression. They may get too much for us and cause depression or a nervous breakdown or they may cause us to live a very low-grade existence that feels stuck. Any method that we use to protect ourselves from our negative emotions like fear, anger, hurt or guilt will almost always backfire on us in some way. We may protect ourselves from being hurt by putting a shell around us and keeping people out. This may cause us to be lonely or rejected and create the very hurt we are protecting against. We may protect ourselves and others from our anger by burying it deep inside but the energy of our anger may attract angry people to us or incite those around us to be angry. We end up being surrounded by the very emotion that we are trying to avoid. We may try to protect ourselves from fear by controlling everyone and everything around us. We may even have to use fear as the weapon of control. We will see mirrored in others the vulnerable, fearful person that we are trying to bury. When we come from a position of fear, we will usually attract the thing we fear most.

In an ideal world the way that we deal with emotions is to let them flow gently from us as and when we feel them. The safe expression of negative emotions means that they have passed through us and are no longer there. When we suppress emotions we are stuck with them. I call this "locking the wolf into the sheep's pen." It makes no sense whatsoever. It would be far more sensible to release the wolf and allow the sheep to be safe. This way we do not hurt ourselves or others nor do we project our feelings onto others or expect them to process them for us. We have to take responsibility for how we feel and choose to let it go. When we allow our emotions to flow, we speed up the process of expelling negative feelings and enjoy the time spent with the positive ones. There may be a backlog of hurt and anger that needs to be cleared but once this is done, we can become conscious and choose how we want to feel in any given moment, no matter what the external provocation may be. Love and joy are our natural state in which to be. When we process our old outdated emotions and dispel the illusions that created them, we cannot help but experience the wonderful feelings constantly.

It is obvious to state that breath is essential to us because without it we would be dead. However, it has many other applications that are nearly as important and will greatly help to improve our quality of life. Not only is it the link between us and physical life, it is also the connection with the emotions, the bridge to the soul or spiritual aspects and it unlocks information stored within the mind. Having said all this, very few of us reap the rewards available to us or even know how to breathe properly.

As with most everything we have looked at in this book, we have unlearned the natural way to breathe and we have to relearn what we did automatically as a baby. If we watch a baby breathing the whole of the stomach and torso will fill with air and expand. As we get older our breath becomes more shallow and many people only use the upper chest while breathing. This means that we are only working at possibly a third of available capacity.

One of the reasons why we learn to shallow breathe is because we do not want to touch our feelings. The centre of the emotions is the solar plexus. We may be very protective of this area. When we breathe into the solar plexus, we connect with whatever feelings may be in residence. If we are not comfortable with this, we will unconsciously find ways in which to avoid accessing them. We may not be aware that we are shallow breathing or the reasons for it. It may seem to us to be a good thing but ultimately it takes us away from dealing with and processing our feelings and has many other repercussions in the process.

In the arena of emotions the breath is not simply essential for accessing our emotions, it is also the tool that we use for releasing them. I always think that the simplest things in life are the best. Most of our emotions spend the majority of time in the suppressed position, in which case we are not in touch or aware of them. Something or someone will often come along and press a button or trigger an emotion to surface where we become aware of it. Most of us will either stay stuck in the emotion until it dissipates and returns to the suppressed position or we try to dump it onto someone else. The moment we feel an emotion we do not like, we can use the breath to expel it from the body once and for all. This does not need to take more than a few minutes to accomplish. We use the breath as a shovel and send it down to the solar plexus and it picks up a load of emotion. We forcibly eject it from the body and then go back for more. Very soon we realise that there is no more of that feeling to let go of and there will be a calm feeling in its place. I cannot stress too strongly the importance of doing this and the incredible results such a simple thing can produce. It can set us free from the tyranny of our negative emotions.

Equally when we feel positive feelings, we can expand these with the breath. Here, instead of putting the emphasis on the out-breath, we use the in-breath to drink in the feeling and capture it as a memory or a moment in time that becomes etched upon our souls.

It is no mistake that the word used for breathing in is also the one used to describe a good idea or creative connection. The word is **INSPIRATION**. This is undoubtedly because the breath is an essential ingredient within the creative process.

The breath has a crucial part to play in the control of pain. We can see this most effectively with childbirth. Our natural reaction when we feel pain is to tense up and stop breathing. This then locks the pain in and prevents it from moving through. When we take conscious breaths, we feel the pain lessening. This can be applied to many painful and chronic conditions. In some cases the pain can disappear altogether. It may be necessary to learn some breathing techniques to help with chronic pain. The more we are able to direct the breath, the greater the effectiveness in dealing with the problem. The great advantage of using the breath as a means of coping with pain is that there are no side effects or addictions and we have it with us whenever it is required.

Breathing plays a large part in accessing information from the brain. Oxygen is needed to feed the brain and very often we do not get enough, either because our breathing is too shallow or the quality of air that we breathe is sub

149

standard due to pollution and lack of trees. We hold an enormous amount of information in our brains, most of which we are not aware that we have. In order to access it we have to send a search engine to retrieve it. We use the breath to do this. I once did this as an experiment when playing a game of Trivial Pursuit with a group of friends. Each time a question was asked that I did not consciously know the answer to, I cleared my mind and breathed until the answer popped into my mind. I was no less shocked than my friends when there was only one question I was unable to answer all evening, well above my usual standard. If we are to operate at an optimal level in our chosen area of work, the breath will play a key role. It focuses and concentrates the mind, it helps to relieve stress and panic, it relaxes the body and maximises the flow of energy to go to where it is needed.

Breath is the essential ingredient needed to access the soul. This is often done through the emotions. Feelings are the language of the soul and this is why we often feel quite teary or emotional when we make that connection. When we ask a question of the higher self or intuition, it is the breath that will put the query out and also bring back the answer. I know for myself that when I feel disconnected or separated from my inner self, it only takes one breath to reconnect me. There is immediately a new sense of peace and positivity that comes in as a result. We do have to be aware of when we have disconnected and allowed the ego to take over the reins. We may have to plug back into our true selves dozens of times a day, depending on how active our egos are.

Breath is an incredible source of energy and nurture for us. We are geared to see food as our main energy source but there are many other means of getting life giving energy. The sun is one such provider. Most of us have more energy and require less food when it is bright and sunny than we do in the dark days of winter. We can also get a vast amount of sustenance through air and our breath. There are even a group of people who have taken this concept to the extreme and are said to live on air without food or water. I am not advocating this but we could utilise this wonderful, readily available and free commodity far more than we do. Once again this can only come about if we learn to breathe in a way that maximises our intake and expels the spent air from our lungs.

The air that we breathe is one of the most valuable commodities available to us and yet we do not fully utilise it. I see a strong correlation between the amount of air that we take into the body and the abundance of the universe that we allow into our lives. Once again I must stress that abundance is not measured by money and the material, it is rather the belief that more than enough is available for our needs, wants and desires, whatever they may be. There is more than enough air for us to breathe, we do not panic about running out or where our next breath is going to come from. Once we start to take in more life giving oxygen, we will probably see a change in our abundance levels.

TIPS FOR BRINGING IN JOY, FUN AND LAUGHTER

1) Look at the extent to which you incorporate joy, fun and laughter into your life. Is it part of all your daily activities or do you keep it just for social and leisure times?

2) If there are mundane or routine things that you do every day, find ways to make them more fun or

enjoyable. For instance, a tedious commute in the car could be lightened by a tape of your favourite book or music. Boring housework could be done by singing or dancing along to the radio. Accounts could be accompanied by a glass of wine or the promise of a reward at the end of it.

3) Notice if you have got into a rut and don't bother to go out or meet people and enjoy yourself. This could also be a sign of low grade depression and old stagnant feelings may need to be released.

4) Make a list of things that you enjoy or give you pleasure. These could be hobbies, interests, social interactions or solitary pastimes. Look at how many of these things you actually fit into your life. Compare this with the amount of time spent doing things you don't enjoy doing. What is this ratio like?

5) If this ratio is under half, actively look for ways to raise your fun quotient. This may mean joining a group, doing classes, inviting friends over or getting out and about and doing things.

6) Try not to wait passively for things and people to come to you but go and create what you want to happen. You may make some mistakes but don't let this put you off.

7) Do you get enjoyment from your work? If not you are either in the wrong job or you may need to learn to see it in a different way or make changes in the way that you do it. Once again this requires an active response and we often will put up with a great deal rather than initiate change. Just think that you may be spending a third or more of your life doing your job and would you choose to spend that much time being miserable or unfulfilled?

8) Do you mix with people who are light and laugh a lot? After you have spent time with your friends do you feel good or do you feel brought down and drained? Sometimes you need to rethink who you choose to spend your time with and whether you have outgrown the friendship and need to move on. Start to mix with people who inspire and uplift you and that you can have a good laugh with.

TIPS FOR IMPROVING BREATH

1) Notice how you breathe. Does it fill the whole body or only the upper chest? Are there times when you hold your breath? Do you have a great deal of tension in the body?

2) When you exhale do you expel all the air from your lungs or just a small amount? Consciously breathe right out and see how much stale air you have sitting in your lungs.

3) Changing your breathing is not something that can happen overnight as your patterns are deeply ingrained. Start by becoming aware of your breath. If you are breathing to full capacity your stomach should inflate when you breathe in. This may feel very unnatural or uncomfortable at first. The muscles will have to be trained to do this naturally.

4) Take time each day to consciously breathe. This does not have to be a chore. It can be done in the car or when watching television. Bring in the new breathing especially when you are feeling stressed or tense.

5) If you can find time in your schedule to go for a walk in nature, this would be very beneficial. The air quality will always be better near trees and plants. Fill your lungs and clear any old stale air out. Focus on

the out-breath rather than the in-breath.

6) Use the breath to release old emotions from the body. Any time you are not feeling good expel the feelings out on the breath.

7) Use the breath to connect with your inner self and your intuition. If you have asked a question, breathe in to receive the answer. The breath can connect you with inspiration so any conundrums can be solved with the aid of deep breathing.

Liz Adamson is available for talks, workshops and intensive 3 hour one to one sessions.

Contact: Flat 3, Hamptons, Hadlow, Tonbridge, Kent, TN11 9SR. Tel 07940 101918.
Email liz@edenbook.co.uk

Also available by Liz Adamson

The 12 Principles of Optimal Living	£7.95
Relationships, A Journey into Wholeness	£7.95
Abundance and Prosperity.	£7.95

The Ultimate Guides to Emotional Freedom

Releasing Anger	£4.95
Releasing Hurt and Sadness	£4.95
Embracing Love	£4.95
Embracing Happiness	£4.95

The Secrets of Optimal Living inspiration cards £7.95

All above titles soon available on high quality CDs

Available from Diviniti Publishing. Tel 01732 220373
Website: www.hypnosisaudio.com

Also available from Diviniti Publishing best selling hypnosis tapes and CDs including:
Complete Relaxation
Lose Weight Now
Heal Your Body and many others.